TEACHER'S BOOK

Louisa May Alcott

retold by Jenny Dooley & Virginia Evans

Published by Express Publishing

Liberty House, New Greenham Park,
Newbury, Berkshire RG19 6HW
Tel: (0044) 1635 817 363 – Fax: (0044) 1635 817 463
e-mail: inquiries@expresspublishing.co.uk
http://www.expresspublishing.co.uk

© Jenny Dooley & Virginia Evans 2009

Colour Illustrations: Victor © Express Publishing, 2009

Design & Illustration © Express Publishing, 2009

Made in EU

All rights reserved. No part of this publication may be reproduced, stored in a retrieval system or transmitted in any form, or by any means, electronic, photocopying or otherwise, without the prior written permission of the publishers.

This book is not meant to be changed in any way.

ISBN 978-1-84862-710-9

Note: Standard American English has been used in the text so that it is consistent with the story. American spelling is also used in the *Analysis* section, where the text is quoted. British English is used everywhere else, keeping consistent with the *Classic Readers Series*.

Contents

Introduction to the Teacher	3
Autobiographical Elements in *Little Women*	15
Questions on Themes, Motifs and Symbols in *Little Women*	16
Themes, Motifs and Symbols in *Little Women* –	
Suggested Answers for the Questions	18
Key to the Activities	20
Final Checks	70
Key to Final Checks	76
THINK! Activities	78
Suggested Answers for the THINK! Activities	80
Game Components	82
Board Game Questions and Suggested Answers	82
Suggested Explanations for the Picture Cards	91
Question Cards	93
Picture Cards	99

Introduction to the Teacher

Why use Readers?

Readers are an important element in any language programme, as they help students broaden their horizons and understand the cultures of other countries and other periods in history. Through reading literature, students become familiar with other points of view and develop their skills of critical thinking and appraisal because they have to consider a book carefully and form their own opinions of it by discussing its strengths and weaknesses. Students become personally involved in the lives of the characters and, for a short time, inhabit a world that is completely different from that of their everyday lives. In this way, they focus on the meanings behind the English language and not merely on its structure (vocabulary, grammar, etc).

The *Express Publishing Classic Readers* series is designed for use at home as well as in class. It can therefore be used alongside any programme, regardless of the time available in the school timetable.

If you decide to use this reader in class, the suggestions in this Teacher's Book will help you with your lesson plans. The activities are optional and can be used in class or given as homework. If you decide to use this Reader for holiday study, you can ask the students to read the book and listen to the recording and do a selection of the activities at home. Later, you can check their answers in class and discuss the main points of the story, eliciting their views on the plot and the characters.

Components

1. The Reader includes:
   a   an abridged version of the classic story.
   b   an *Introductory Lesson*, which is intended to stimulate

students' interest and create a positive atmosphere so that they become involved in the story. Students discuss a set of questions based on the cover, chapter titles, characters, pictures, etc. The author's biography is also included to set the story in the right historical context, which helps students make intelligent guesses about what to expect in the story and why it was written.

c an *Activities* section, which presents a variety of optional tasks. These tasks provide an opportunity for students to check their comprehension, discuss the issues raised in the story, practise the language they have learnt and extend their knowledge in a meaningful way.

d two final *Projects* based on the main theme of the story. These projects aim to further explore the main issues raised, or the characters and the plot of the book. This can be done in many ways, e.g. by students comparing a situation to their own experiences and culture, or by writing reviews and making evaluations through questionnaires, etc.

e an alphabetical *Word List*, which the students can turn into a glossary by writing a definition or translation for each item.

2 *The Teacher's Book* includes:

a a *Suggested Lesson Plan*, offering ideas on how to use the reader in combination with the activities in class.

b *Supplementary Activities for Readers* that can be used with any title and with minimum preparation on behalf of the teacher. These activities are also optional and aim to further extend students' understanding of literature, develop their critical thinking skills and increase their interest in the story.

c information on autobiographical elements in *Little Women*.

d information on themes, motifs and symbols in Little *Women*, together with activities and suggested answers.

e optional photocopiable *THINK! Activities* and suggested answers.

f the *Key to the Activities* presented in the Reader.

g suggested answers for the projects.

h two photocopiable versions of a *Final Check* that can be used as a means of evaluating students' knowledge and understanding of the story and the language they have acquired by reading it.

i the game cards for the *Board Game* that accompanies the Teacher's Book.

❸ *A Board Game* in the form of a poster that can be used to review the story and the language learnt. This poster accompanies the Teacher's Book.

❹ *The audio CD* includes a fully dramatised audio version of the story. This helps students become more involved in the story, as well as providing a model for the appropriate pronunciation and intonation of the English language.

Suggested Lesson Plan for the Following Lessons

▶ *Warm-up*

As a warm-up, you may wish to write on the board either the title of the chapter or some words/phrases (i.e. five to six key sentences or ten to fifteen key words) taken from the *Word List* and ask students to predict what is going to happen. Try not to allow more than five minutes for this short discussion. Alternatively, you may ask them to brainstorm on one issue dealt with in the respective chapter, e.g. *Little Women* Chapter 5: "Meg Becomes a Lady". Write the key word 'lady' on the board, and ask students to tell you what words come to mind when they think of this. Write down all their suggestions.

▶ *Presentation and Practice*

There are two ways to present and practise each chapter: by listening or reading. The steps for these are as follows:

5

LISTENING

a *Listening for gist:* Play the recording. Students listen and compare the action in the story to their predictions in the warm-up stage.

b *Listening for specific information:* refer students to the *Activities* section in the Reader. Ask students to read the *Comprehension* questions and underline all key words, i.e. all the words and phrases that will give them an idea of what to listen for. Ask students what kinds of words/phrases they may hear in the recording that are associated with the key words. Play the recording while students take notes in their notebooks. You may choose to divide the *Comprehension* questions between different groups, so that each student does not deal with more than two or three questions. Discuss the answers with the class.

READING

a *Reading for gist:* Students read the chapter quickly and compare the action in the story to their predictions in the warm-up stage.

b *Reading for specific information:* refer students to the *Activities* section in the Reader. Ask students to read the *Comprehension* questions and underline all key words, i.e. all the words and phrases that will give them an idea of what to look for. Ask students what kinds of words/phrases they may come across in the chapter that are associated with the key words. Students read and underline the parts of the text that answer the questions. You may choose to divide the *Comprehension* questions between different groups, so that each student does not deal with more than two or three questions. Discuss the answers with the class. Encourage students to use their own words and justify their answers.

▶ *Discussion*
To personalise the text, refer students to the *What do you think?* questions in the *Activities* section. These questions will generate discussion on the issues presented in the chapter and help students to identify with the story. This will ensure a more holistic learning experience. These questions can also be used as a springboard for further discussion. Encourage your students to discuss their views openly and accept all answers provided they are well justified.

▶ *Language Practice*
To provide practice of the language in each chapter as well as helping students focus on the literary analysis of the text (working with words, collocations, metaphors, similes, etc), refer students to the *Language Practice* tasks in the *Activities* section. These tasks can be assigned for homework and discussed in class during the next session. However, you should make sure that students understand what they have to do in each task beforehand. Ask students to read the instructions in class and then do the first question as an example. You may wish to refer them to a dictionary for any unknown vocabulary.

▶ *Extension*
As an extension, there may be one or more different types of tasks at the end of each *Activities* chapter, which may also be used as warm-up activities at the beginning of the next chapter.

a **What happens next?:** These tasks aim to enhance students' motivation and interest by using what they know about the story so far and extending this information so as to make assumptions based on textual information, pictures and their own evaluation of the story.

b **Guess the meaning:** This task is designed to help students practise reading a short paragraph, unrelated to the main Reader, and inferring the meaning of words or phrases they will come across in the following chapter. This can be assigned for homework or used as a vocabulary warm-up at the beginning of the next session.

c *Vocabulary:* These exercises help students to learn new words and better understand more specific concepts within a sentence or passage. They are in the form of crosswords, sentence completion, antonyms/synonyms, matching, collocation construction, etc.

d *Culture Corner:* Identifying and understanding the cultural concepts within a story is important for students to understand the story itself. By analysing situations and historical moments, they can better differentiate between yesterday's and today's important social developments.

e *Think!:* These tasks encourage students to put themselves into similar situations to the ones presented in the story. This way they better understand the plot, characters and the author's intentions. Posing questions, having group discussions, imagining hypothetical situations, ordering events and acting out scenarios can all help in this process.

f *What's the moral?:* Evaluating the various situations the characters are involved in can lead students to better understand the meaning of the story and the lesson(s) it teaches about life.

g After reading the last chapter, you may wish to present one of the *Projects* included in the Reader.

h Throughout the study of the Reader, you may wish to use the *Supplementary Activities for Readers.*

Final Check

The *Final Check* quizzes in this Teacher's Book are optional and designed to revise the whole book in terms of plot, language and literary analysis. Through this *Final Check*, you can evaluate students' knowledge of the plotline, their listening skills, the language they have learnt and their paraphrasing skills, as well as identifying their strengths and weaknesses. Alternatively, you may wish to enhance their autonomy by photocopying the key to the quiz and allowing students to assess themselves.

There are two versions of the same *Final Check* quiz so that students can be divided into two groups to do the respective quizzes. You may also wish to create your own quizzes using familiar items (vocabulary, comprehension questions, etc) from the *Activities* section. In this case, try not to compile more than 20 questions in each quiz so that students can complete it in no more than 10 to 15 minutes.

Supplementary Activities for Readers

1 Character Lines

Aims:
1. To provide speaking practice by generating discussion about the main characters of the Reader.
2. To develop students' critical thinking skills.

Preparation: Select 3 or 4 characters that students have come across in the story and 3 pairs of opposite adjectives that may describe their personalities.

Materials: The board and the Reader.

Description:
1. Write the names of the characters you have selected, e.g. *Little Women*: Jo, Meg, Beth, Amy.
2. Below the names draw 3 lines and on each side of each line write the adjectives – strong/weak, caring/spoilt, shy/outgoing – as shown:

Jo	Meg	Beth	Amy
strong			weak
caring			spoilt
shy			outgoing

3. Ask students to copy this diagram into their notebooks and then place each of the characters at the point on the line they think he/she belongs.
4. Each student expresses their opinion in class, justifying it by referring to the Reader if necessary.

9

2 Trip to Fantasy-Land
      Aims: 1 To foster personal involvement in the story thus helping students 'inhabit' the text.
                    2 To raise students' motivation and interest in the story.
                    3 To practise listening for general understanding.
      Preparation: Select a chapter from the Reader with a few emotional highlights and vivid descriptions and the best points at which to stop.
      Materials: A CD player and the audio CD of the story.
      Description: 1 Explain to students that they will listen to a chapter. Tell them to keep their eyes closed while listening and imagine that they are actually inside each scene as witnesses.
                    2 Play the chapter. When you reach the first stopping point, pause the recording.
                    3 Ask various students to describe what they see/hear/smell or how they feel. Allow them to improvise by adding their own details to the story.
                    4 Play the recording again, until the next stopping point.

3 Wall Chart
      Aims: 1 To practise summarising main points.
                    2 To practise students' evaluation skills.
      Preparation: None.
      Materials: One big sheet of paper that can be used as a poster and several different coloured markers.
      Description: 1 Explain to students that you are going to make an evaluation poster for the Reader you are studying, which you are going to have to fill in every time you finish a chapter.

2. Draw a grid of 11 rows x 4 columns on the sheet of paper. In each cell of the first row, write the following: the title of the reader, e.g. *Little Women*, the headings "Plot", "What we liked" and "What we didn't like". You may wish to let students decorate the poster with illustrations.
3. In the first column write the chapter numbers and titles.
4. When you finish studying the first chapter, ask students to name the 5 most important events in it. Write them in a list on the board. Allow students to debate the importance of each event.
5. Ask students what they liked/didn't like about the plot of the chapter. This could be anything, e.g. how Jo reacted when she found out what Laurie's secret was, etc.
6. Assign one student to fill in the cells for the first chapter with everything you have discussed. A different student should fill in the chart for each chapter.

4 Role Play

Aims:
1. To practise speaking in long and short turns within a given context.
2. To practise anticipation of plot.
3. To promote group/pairwork.

Preparation: None.

Materials: A *"Guess what happens next"* activity from the *Activities* section of the reader.

Description:
1. After having completed a *"Guess what happens next"* task from the *Activities* section, divide the class into groups or pairs.
2. Students within the same group/pair decide on a common scenario for the continuation of the story.

3 Students assume a role from their own scenarios and practise a dialogue based on it.

4 Students act out their scenarios in class.

5 Time/Place Research

Aims:
1 To encourage students to carry out research on the era and the place, in order to gain a better understanding of the story.
2 To promote learner autonomy.

Preparation: Select a few resources (e.g. encyclopaedias, magazine articles, etc) to present to the class, which will provide information on the time period and place of the story. For example, you need to find information on aspects such as: the clothing, buildings, schooling system, food and professions of the era. If Internet access is available, you may wish to carry out a short search and print out a few articles as well.

Materials: A large sheet of paper, the resources you have selected, and the Reader.

Description:
1 Ask your students to use the Reader (text and pictures) to make a list of things they know about the time and place of the story.
2 Explain to your students that you are going to make a poster with visual and textual information they collect about the relevant time or place (e.g. the civil war era in America for *Little Women*).
3 Allow students 20 minutes to go through the material you have brought in and keep notes about any other information they obtain.
4 Encourage your students to continue their research at home and bring in more information or pictures they can draw of objects, houses, clothes, etc of the period.

5 In the next lesson, compile all the information the students bring in, along with their drawings or photos to make a poster. Allow your students some time to decide how to put everything together and to complete the layout.

Board Game

Another enjoyable way to revise the book is through the *Classic Readers Board Game* which accompanies this Teacher's Book. It should be played after the completion of the story. The *Game Components* are included in this Teacher's Book. The board game is a wonderful way to motivate students to refer back to the story, thus enhancing their knowledge of English.

Game Components
The following game components are included in this Teacher's Book:
- A list with more than 100 questions on the characters, the action, the places and the language presented in the story. Suggested answers are also included.
- 12 cards with a set of 5 questions on each one.
- 18 picture cards showing items related to the story.

How to play
1 Cut out all the picture cards and the question cards for this game.
2 Divide the class into two teams, A and B.
3 Present the board game to the students. You may either put the poster on a table and invite students to form a circle around it, or put it up on the board using blu-tack. Elicit the features they see in it (e.g. express train, railway station, collapsed bridge, flooded tracks, broken-down car, workmen on track, etc).
4 Point to the red squares along the track. Explain that each time they land on one of those squares, they must answer a question about the book, either on the plot, the characters

or the language they have seen in it. If no one in the team knows the answer, the team misses a turn. It is important that the question is answered, however, so you may ask the other team if they know it or answer yourself. Hold up the list with the questions for these squares, but do not let them see what the questions are.

5 Point to the five disasters on the board game (collapsed bridge, flood, breakdown, workmen on track, landslide). Explain that each time they land on the square before the disaster, they have to answer FIVE mixed questions (from a *Question Card*) in order to continue. If they do not, they will miss two turns. Again, make sure the students hear the correct answer before the game continues. Hold up the *Question Cards* as well, but do not let them see what the questions are.

6 Point to the starred squares between the start and finish of the game. Take the *Picture Cards* and show a couple of them to the students. Shuffle them and put them (face down) on the picture card box. Explain that as they pass over these squares, they have to pick up the top card and keep it until the end of the game. When they land on square 79, the team will have to explain how the items depicted on the cards they have collected are related to the story. If they are unable to do so, they lose.

7 Use two different items from the classroom as counters for each team (e.g. a sharpener and an eraser). If you choose to play the game with the poster put up on the board, you may use two magnets, or differently coloured blu-tack, as counters. Bring a dice or make one using a pencil with six sides, on each of which you write the numbers 1-6. The teams will move according to the number that comes up when they roll the pencil or the dice.

8 Tell students that each time they are asked a question, the team will have to decide which team member will provide the answer. Make sure that as many students as possible get a chance to speak.

9 Roll the 'dice'. The team with the highest number begins.

Autobiographical Elements in *Little Women*

The March family is similar to Louisa May Alcott's own family in many ways. There were four Alcott girls who enjoyed putting on plays just as the March girls do. The incident at the beginning of the book, where they give their breakfast to a poor family at Christmas, is also based on a real-life incident.

Meg March is Alcott's older sister Anna. Anna, like Meg, was attracted to wealthy luxurious living. In spite of that, she married a poor man, which is what Meg goes on to do in *Good Wives*, the sequel to *Little Women*.

Jo, the second sister, is a portrayal of Louisa May Alcott herself. A keen writer, like her creator, Jo is given a tomboyish character which reflects the author's feelings about her own situation. In Alcott's day, writing for your living was something a man usually did; women were expected to raise a family and look after the home.

The third Alcott sister, Elizabeth, is the model for Beth. Elizabeth was musical, as is Beth, and her portrait was kept near the Alcott family piano. The piano is Beth's beloved instrument in *Little Women*. Amy's name is an anagram of the name May. May was the youngest Alcott sister and was talented at drawing, just as her counterpart Amy is.

Mr Alcott experienced difficulties with money, and his wife worked hard to support him and keep the family together. The same thing happens with Mr and Mrs March in the novel. In real life, Louisa helped her parents by taking teaching and sewing jobs at the age of 15. This reminds us of Jo's and Meg's efforts to earn money for the family by looking after Aunt March and the King children respectively.

It seems there was an emotional distance between Louisa May Alcott and her father. Louisa had a strong and independent personality like Jo. Mr Alcott wanted his daughter to be milder and more ladylike. This distance has been suggested as the reason why Louisa Alcott cannot write a fully developed father figure. Instead, Mr March is fighting in the war, away from the main action of the book.

Questions on Themes, Motifs and Symbols in *Little Women*

Read the text and answer the questions.

Themes

Themes are the basic ideas contained in a novel. They often have meaning and importance for mankind generally and not just within the novel. In 19th century America, women were traditionally expected to marry and provide a comfortable home for their families. In *Little Women*, the heroines do not always directly follow this tradition. Jo struggles between what society expects of her and what she really wants for herself, that is, to become a writer. Normally young ladies worried about things like being in fashion and finding a marriage partner to settle down with. The Moffat sisters are a good example of this. Jo is the complete opposite. She is a tomboy, neglects her appearance and wants to earn her own living. The contrast between the Moffats and the Marches also serves as a way of emphasising the importance of paying more attention to the inner self than to ephemeral things like wealth and appearance. Unlike the Moffat girls, the March sisters constantly try to become better people and dedicate themselves to useful work. The 19th century Puritan work ethic stressed the importance of doing useful productive work. The Puritans were a religious movement who believed that work was not just a means of earning your living but was also a sacred expression of inner goodness. In this matter, *Little Women* is in strong agreement. It is only by doing work, either for a living or to help the family, that the March girls can feel fulfilled and happy. Not working results in feelings of guilt and remorse.

Motifs
Motifs are structures or patterns that are repeated in a novel. They help the author to develop the main ideas or themes.
Music is a significant motif in Little Women, indicating a character's degree of conformity to traditionally accepted stereotypes. Learning to sing and play a musical instrument was considered important for young girls, who were expected to fulfil their feminine duties. They developed their musical talents as a hobby and in order to provide entertainment at home and amongst friends. In the novel, the more musically talented a girl is, the more ladylike she is. Shy Beth, who adores the piano, is clearly a sharp contrast to Jo here. Another significant motif is that of teaching. Quite a number of the novel's characters are involved in teaching in some way, both giving and learning lessons. This is appropriate in a didactic novel where the reader is intended to learn from its lessons.

Symbols
Symbols are concrete images which are used to represent abstract ideas.
In Little Women, the symbol of burning represents anger and a writer's power. Amy burns Jo's stories in anger after Jo refuses to let her come to the play. Jo wears a party dress with a burn mark on it; this symbolises her fiery temperament and powerful will. Unlike Meg, who is vain about her appearance, Jo doesn't mind wearing a damaged dress to a party, refusing to conform to her conventional female role.

1. Look back at the story. What examples in the text illustrate the importance of doing work?
2. What parts of the story refer to the subject of teaching?
3. Can you think of any other things in Little Women that act as symbols? Justify your answer.

Themes, Motifs and Symbols in *Little Women* – Suggested Answers for the Questions

1. - p. 9: "… I hate working, but I will try to change."
   - p. 20: 'All too soon, the holidays were over and it was time for the March sisters to return to their work.' / '… the two eldest girls had begged to be allowed to help support the family. Meg earned a small salary as a nursery governess at the King family.' / 'Jo looked after Aunt March, who was old and lived alone.' / 'Devouring every single line or verse, Jo's ambition was to achieve something important one day.'
   - p. 44: '… they all decided to keep busy until Mother returned. Meg went to work at the King house, Jo went to look after Aunt March, and Beth and Amy helped Hannah around the house.' / 'Only Beth continued to work hard at home. She did all the little chores around the house and even found time for others.'
   - p. 49: 'She also showed her mother the turquoise ring that Aunt March had given her for all her hard work and good behavior.'
   - p. 59: "I remember when this hand was white and smooth, and you wanted to keep it that way. It was very pretty then, but I prefer it like this. It shows that you have worked hard for your family."

2. - p. 20: 'Meg earned a small salary as a nursery governess at the King family.' / 'Mr. March had given Beth lessons until he went away to fight in the war.'
   - p. 37: 'Meg … often chatted with Laurie's tutor, Mr. Brooke …'

3. Slippers are a recurring object in the novel. Jo suggests buying Mother a new pair of slippers for Christmas to replace her old ones. Beth makes Mr. Laurence a pair of slippers, a present which seems to really touch him, to thank him for his generosity in giving her a piano. Slippers symbolise the comfort of home and show the giver cares about the comfort of others. They also represent warmth and leisure, which is what the characters long for in this troubled time.

Gloves are another recurring object symbolising women's adherence to the moral principles of the time. Meg says a lady must always wear gloves when she dances. Jo, on the other hand, defies decorum, suggesting they wear only one glove each since her gloves are ruined. Being rebellious, she cannot confine herself to rules and restrictions. When Laurie sees Meg's glove in Mr Brooke's pocket, he finds it romantic. Giving away a glove means leaving one's hand exposed, which was quite bold for a lady to do in terms of decency.

Hair is another symbol of propriety and ladylike behaviour. Meg has her hair curled for the New Year's Eve ball and tied in a ribbon after it's burnt so that the damage doesn't show. Jo wears hairpins that stick into her head and make her feel uncomfortable. Her discomfort is indicative of her attitude to convention in contrast to Meg, who pays great attention to such matters. It is Meg who has her hair curled at the Moffat house and Meg again who is shocked to see Jo's hair gone.

Key to the Activities

Introductory Lesson

1 **(Suggested answers)** The picture is probably of a mother and her daughters seated comfortably at home around the piano, playing and singing. They look like nicely-dressed, educated women. They must be in their home and they seem to be feeling happy. Perhaps they are celebrating a special event or enjoying their favourite pastime.

2 A "little woman" is a young lady. This title seems reflective of the fact that the four sisters are young, but act like mature, respectful and independent ladies. Perhaps they are going through a difficult time or a crucial stage in their life and have to grow up abruptly. The term "little women" might also reflect women's role at the time, suggesting that women were rather restricted, having to conform to particular ways of behaviour and accept certain limitations.

3 Vanity makes a person take great pride in themselves and their appearance. As a result, they tend to be superficial, focusing on trivialities and missing the essence of things. Vain people can be snobbish, thinking they are superior to others, when in reality they are very shallow because they only care about the way they look.
Hot temper is a major character flaw, as it prevents people from thinking calmly but rather leads them to rash, thoughtless action. A hot-tempered person is very likely to make the wrong decision, as what urges them is anger and not reason. Driven by anger, they cannot but have poor judgment.
Shyness can be a serious obstacle for someone, as shy people are hesitant about communicating with others. They tend to be alone, relying on themselves, and find it hard to socialise

with people. Shyness can prevent a person from taking action and advancing in life, due to lack of courage and boldness. Selfishness makes people only interested in themselves. Selfish people are self-centred, paying attention to their needs and ignoring everyone else. They can be so self-absorbed that it is impossible for them to sympathise with others and offer them their help and support.

4   The hardships the March family is experiencing will probably make them stronger and wiser and bring them closer. After Mr March returns home, the family will be united and live happily.

5   1   She was born on 29 November 1832.
    2   She had three sisters.
    3   Her father and family friends taught her.
    4   She started working at a young age because her family was poor.
    5   Her first book was called *Flower Fables*.
    6   She worked as a nurse.
    7   It was published in 1868.
    8   She was 55 years old when she died.

Chapter 1 - A Merry Christmas

Comprehension

1 F	3 F	5 F	7 T	9 F
2 T	4 T	6 F	8 T	10 T

What do you think?

A   (Suggested answers)
    1   The March family proves to be very compassionate and caring, sympathising with people who suffer and are not

as advantaged as they are. All four sisters are willing to follow their mother's advice and not buy Christmas presents this year. This way they show their support for the men who are fighting in the war and are not having a merry holiday. The March sisters' kind feelings are also reflected in their decision to spend all their money on presents for their mother and not to buy anything for themselves. The girls' promise to their father also shows their kindness. Knowing that he is going through a hard time, while they enjoy the warmth of their house, they decide to become better people. Mrs March also proves to be very caring when she buys her daughters small Christmas presents, taking their gloom away. However, the family's altruistic feelings are mostly reflected in their decision to give their breakfast to a poor family who is in need. It is the girls' kindness that makes Mr Laurence reward them, although at times it may not be obvious that a kind act is rewarded.

2 It must definitely be hard for the March family to be separated, especially at this time of year. Mrs March and the girls must feel sad at the thought that their beloved husband and father is away, risking his life in the war. His absence may have shaken their sense of security and stability within the family. Now they have to provide everything themselves, as they have no one else to rely on. Being the head of the family, Mr March should be there to keep everyone united. Now that he is away, his wife must make up for his absence by also being a father to the girls. She has to be strong and positive so that her daughters won't lose heart but go on living as normal a life as possible.

3 In his letter, Mr March does not talk about the dangers and troubles of the war but about his love for his family. This is very thoughtful and brave of him, considering that he is going through a very difficult situation and would have every right to complain about it. Instead, he writes a cheerful, hopeful letter that brings his daughters tears of joy. This is what makes

them want to prove that they are worthy of their father's love. Amy will try to be less selfish, Meg is determined to enjoy working more and Jo promises to become a little woman. As for Beth, she confirms her sisters' promises by playing the old piano. The girls' attitude indicates their great love for their father. It also proves that, despite their young age, they are mature and sensible enough to make good decisions.

4 Modern societies lack a lot of moral values that people used to appreciate in the past. Standards are different today, as people are more interested in material possessions than human relationships. Everyone is more self-centred, absorbed in their own lives and problems, and people don't take time to care about others. Even if they are willing to do so, their hectic schedules won't let them. Therefore, people like the Marches are rare to find today.

B (**Suggested answers**)
1 It is very difficult for Jo, who is still very young, to accept the reality of the war. Her father is away risking his life, and the rest of the family has to work to provide food and the bare necessities. This means that this year no one will get any Christmas presents. It is a hard fact to accept, since Christmas is especially enjoyed by the young ones.
2 Mrs Hummel's reaction to the Marches' benevolent deed shows how grateful and lucky she feels. It is not common to see people giving away their food in times of war, so Mrs Hummel can only see this as a gift from heaven. The fact that the March family can sympathise with people in need at this difficult time shows strength of character and generosity.
3 Beth appears to be very sensitive to other people's feelings, as she wants to send the flowers that she and her sisters received from Mr Laurence on Christmas night to their father. Mr March is off at the war, so he can't be having a nice Christmas. He won't enjoy a homemade meal in the company of his family. For him, this Christmas will be sad and lonely, and Beth's recognition of this proves how considerate she is.

Language Practice

I 1 c   2 f   3 b   4 a   5 d   6 e

II 1 rehearse   4 are suffering   7 whispers
   2 reward   5 pleasurable
   3 strikes   6 servant

Analysis

You may wish to help Ss analyse the meaning and the underlying implications of the following excerpts after the chapter has been read and the comprehension questions discussed.

- p.8: *"It's not fair! Some girls have lots of pretty things, and other girls have nothing at all."* Amy shares Jo's bad mood as she cannot help complaining about their difficult situation this Christmas. She also appears to be envious of other girls who have everything they need. It is difficult for someone at such a young age to miss out on the pleasures of Christmas.

- p.8: *"But we've got Father and Mother, and each other."* Beth is doing her best to make her sisters cheer up a little. Things are not as bad as they seem. They may not have money this year but they still have each other, and this should be enough. In contrast to her sisters, Beth sees things in a very mature way. What matters at this difficult time is not material possessions but unity in the family.

- p.8: *"We haven't got Father. We won't have him for a long time."* Despite Beth's positive attitude, Jo remains pessimistic. She wants her father to be with them physically and not mentally. Whatever Beth says, his absence is so unbearable that nothing can console Jo.

- p.8: *"Mother suggested not having presents this Christmas because it will be a hard winter for everyone. She thinks it is wrong to spend money on pleasurable things when the men are suffering in the war. We can't do much to help them, but we should think of them, and not of ourselves."* Mother's words reflect her benevolent nature. At this hard time they should not think of themselves but those fighting in the war. When Mr March joins the army, Mrs March and her daughters are left with the difficult task of supporting themselves. However, they still enjoy the safety of their house. The girls' father, on the other hand, as well as everyone fighting, is risking his life away from home. It would be selfish of the girls to care about Christmas presents when so many people lack even the basic necessities. Apart from being considerate and kind, Mrs March also proves to be a good mother providing her daughters with moral guidance.

- p.9: *"I know! Let's each buy something for Mother and not buy anything for ourselves."* Beth once again shows her sensitive, kind nature. She is very altruistic and generous, as she is willing to go without a Christmas present so that her mother can have one instead. Especially the fact that Mrs March needs a new pair of slippers makes Beth even more determined to do something nice for her mother.
- p.9: *'It was a cheerful, hopeful letter, with little news of the dangers and troubles of the war. Instead, Mr. March wrote of his love for his wife and his daughters.'* Mr March appears to be surprisingly considerate in his letter to his family. He doesn't want them to be burdened with his problems or feel worried about the dangers of the war. Instead, he gives them hope and lifts their spirits with his cheerful letter.
- p.12: *"Merry Christmas, girls! I've been visiting the Hummel family. They live near us and they are very poor. They have neither food nor fire. Will you give them your breakfast as a Christmas present?"* Mrs March once again proves to be very kind and considerate, sympathising with her poor neighbours. This is not a time of abundance for anyone, yet Mrs March is willing to share what she has, setting an example for her daughters.
- p.13: *"No. It is from old Mr. Laurence next door. He heard about your kindness this morning and wanted to reward you."* It seems that Mrs March is not the only one with kind feelings. Mr Laurence proves to be as kind-hearted and generous when he acknowledges the March girls' benevolent nature and rewards them.

- p.13: *"He's the Laurence boy's grandfather. Once, our cat ran away, and the Laurence boy brought her back. We just chatted over the fence. I wish I could get to know him."* Jo expresses her interest in the Laurence boy, who seems to be as well mannered as his grandfather. She also appears to be sociable and outgoing, not hesitating to make friends with a boy.

Chapter 2 - The Laurence Boy

Comprehension

1 They are invited to a party at Mrs Gardiner's house on New Year's Eve.
2 Jo's dress has a burn and a tear in the back and her gloves are stained with lemonade.
3 She suggests they each wear one good glove and carry a stained one.
4 Meg's hair is burnt.
5 They tie her hair in a ribbon so that the damage doesn't show too much.
6 They feel nervous but they soon begin chatting with other guests of their age.
7 Meg's lectures to Jo are about the proper ways of being a lady.
8 Jo hides because she feels suddenly shy when she sees a boy approaching her to invite her to dance.
9 She meets the Laurence boy.
10 Her shoe turns and she twists her ankle.

What do you think?

A **(Suggested answers)**
1 Meg and Jo seem to be completely different characters. Meg's behaviour is more typical of a girl, as she is interested

in looking pretty and behaving like a lady. She is concerned about what to wear to the party and is quick to come up with a solution to Jo's problem with her clothes. Meg is really interested in her appearance and even sounds vain. However, she admits her vanity. She puts so much effort into styling her hair, but when the whole effort ends up in disaster, she does not complain. Instead, she says she shouldn't bother about these things so much. The fact that she admits her vanity seems to counterbalance her behaviour, making her appear funny rather than bad.

Jo, on the other hand, is more like a tomboy. She doesn't care about girlish things and sees everything her sister lectures her about as insignificant. The fact that her dress and gloves are ruined shows that she doesn't care for clothes or dressing up. Jo wants to be herself and finds pleasure in joining the boys rather than the girls at the party. She spends the whole evening talking to the Laurence boy and doesn't worry about being ladylike like her sister. I like Jo best, because she isn't afraid to be herself, even if others might not approve.

2 Our appearance reflects parts of our personality, as it displays our tastes and, to some extent, our attitudes towards life. Therefore, it is important that we don't neglect the way we look. A decent appearance indicates respect for ourselves and the people around us. However, we shouldn't worry about our appearance too much, as we may run the risk of becoming vain. We should always remember that appearance isn't everything. What is much more important is personality. It is our values and principles, not our clothes, that define who we are.

3 Meg's advice to Jo probably sounds old-fashioned today, as they lived with a different code of behaviour and ethics. Our modern lifestyle dictates different rules of conduct, and what seems proper to Meg is most likely to appear silly or exaggerated to us. Considering the ways people

entertain themselves and dress today, one would say there is total lack of decorum. However, we should always behave properly when circumstances call for it and not reject manners in the name of modernity and progress.

B **(Suggested answers)**
1 Meg's instructions to Jo reflect her attitude towards social conventions. To her, it is very important for a girl to be ladylike and well-mannered. In contrast to Jo, who doesn't care about etiquette, Meg takes pains to appear respectable, as she wishes to be socially acceptable.
2 Meg seems to reach a point of self-realisation when she admits that she deserves what has happened to her. Worrying about her appearance so much was obviously not a wise thing to do, as she has only made it worse. The fact that she acknowledges her mistake means that she admits her vanity.

Language Practice

1 at	4 in	7 up	10 on
2 for	5 for	8 of	
3 towards	6 to	9 of	

Think (Suggested answer)

Dear Father,

Happy New Year! I hope you are well.

Meg and I had the most fantastic time on New Year's Eve. We were invited to a party at Mrs Gardiner's house. You can imagine Meg's excitement from the moment we received the invitation and her determination to look like a little woman – and she insisted on turning me into one too! The atmosphere at home on New Year's Eve afternoon is hard to describe in words; finding the right things to wear, doing Meg's hair – which was a complete disaster! – and Meg lecturing me on how to behave like a lady. Anyway, the party itself made up for all our effort. Meg enjoyed the girlish gossip while I had a great time talking

to the boys. You'll never believe who I met – the Laurence boy! He is so nice and friendly. We spent the whole night talking, and he even offered to take us back home in his grandfather's carriage when Meg twisted her ankle while dancing. I'd like to see him again and get to know him better.
Please write soon. We all miss you.
With all my love,
Jo

Analysis

You may wish to help Ss analyse the meaning and the underlying implications of the following excerpts after the chapter has been read and the comprehension questions discussed.

- p.14: *"Look, Jo! You and I have been invited to a party at Mrs. Gardiner's house on New Year's Eve!"* Meg cannot hide her excitement at the thought of attending a party. She appears to be very sociable and outgoing, and the prospect of having something to look forward to at this difficult time is hopeful and reassuring.
- p.14: *'Meg was not very happy about this idea. She was proud of her tiny hands and did not want Jo's big hand to stretch her glove. However, she didn't want her sister to be seen without gloves, so she agreed to the plan.'* Meg once again appears to be vain, as she is interested in herself and her appearance. However, she is not selfish. Thinking it would be inappropriate for Jo to be seen at the ball without gloves, she agrees to give her one of hers even though she is afraid Jo's hand will stretch it.
- p.15: *'Eventually, Meg and Jo were ready to go, although they were not very comfortable. Jo's hairpins were sticking into her head and Meg's shoes were too tight, but the girls looked elegant, and that was the main thing.'* The girls are having a hard time getting used to their outfits. In their effort to become presentable for the party, they end up feeling uncomfortable. However, they have no choice but to endure their situation, since what is most important is for them to look elegant and ladylike.

- p.16: *"Fine, thank you, Mr. Laurence; but I'm not Miss March. I'm just Jo."* Jo's words confirm that she is not interested in formalities. She wants to be herself and she is very spontaneous when she meets Laurie. She makes him feel comfortable, encouraging friendly conversation right from the beginning.
- p.17: *"My stupid shoe turned and I twisted my ankle. I can hardly stand. I don't know how I'm going to get home. And Hannah will be here any minute now."* Following the incident with her hair, Meg is having another painful experience. This time, she is suffering because of her uncomfortable shoes, which have caused her to sprain her ankle. In contrast to Jo, who is enjoying herself throughout the party, Meg seems to be trapped in her vanity.

Chapter 3 - A New Friendship

Comprehension

1 property
2 grumpy
3 shy
4 drawing
5 adventures
6 statues
7 slippers
8 granddaughter

What do you think?

(Suggested answers)

1 Studying at home can be relaxing, since no amount of time is spent on catching a train or bus to school in the morning. In fact, a student who studies at home can adjust their schedule to their convenience. Another big advantage of studying at home is that one can study at their own pace, without having to catch up with other students who probably have different skills and abilities. Besides, a student can be undisturbed at

to the boys. You'll never believe who I met – the Laurence boy! He is so nice and friendly. We spent the whole night talking, and he even offered to take us back home in his grandfather's carriage when Meg twisted her ankle while dancing. I'd like to see him again and get to know him better.

Please write soon. We all miss you.

With all my love,

Jo

Analysis

You may wish to help Ss analyse the meaning and the underlying implications of the following excerpts after the chapter has been read and the comprehension questions discussed.

- p.14: *"Look, Jo! You and I have been invited to a party at Mrs. Gardiner's house on New Year's Eve!"* Meg cannot hide her excitement at the thought of attending a party. She appears to be very sociable and outgoing, and the prospect of having something to look forward to at this difficult time is hopeful and reassuring.

- p.14: *'Meg was not very happy about this idea. She was proud of her tiny hands and did not want Jo's big hand to stretch her glove. However, she didn't want her sister to be seen without gloves, so she agreed to the plan.'* Meg once again appears to be vain, as she is interested in herself and her appearance. However, she is not selfish. Thinking it would be inappropriate for Jo to be seen at the ball without gloves, she agrees to give her one of hers even though she is afraid Jo's hand will stretch it.

- p.15: *'Eventually, Meg and Jo were ready to go, although they were not very comfortable. Jo's hairpins were sticking into her head and Meg's shoes were too tight, but the girls looked elegant, and that was the main thing.'* The girls are having a hard time getting used to their outfits. In their effort to become presentable for the party, they end up feeling uncomfortable. However, they have no choice but to endure their situation, since what is most important is for them to look elegant and ladylike.

- p.16: *"Fine, thank you, Mr. Laurence; but I'm not Miss March. I'm just Jo."* Jo's words confirm that she is not interested in formalities. She wants to be herself and she is very spontaneous when she meets Laurie. She makes him feel comfortable, encouraging friendly conversation right from the beginning.
- p.17: *"My stupid shoe turned and I twisted my ankle. I can hardly stand. I don't know how I'm going to get home. And Hannah will be here any minute now."* Following the incident with her hair, Meg is having another painful experience. This time, she is suffering because of her uncomfortable shoes, which have caused her to sprain her ankle. In contrast to Jo, who is enjoying herself throughout the party, Meg seems to be trapped in her vanity.

Chapter 3 - A New Friendship

Comprehension

1. property
2. grumpy
3. shy
4. drawing
5. adventures
6. statues
7. slippers
8. granddaughter

What do you think?

(Suggested answers)

1. Studying at home can be relaxing, since no amount of time is spent on catching a train or bus to school in the morning. In fact, a student who studies at home can adjust their schedule to their convenience. Another big advantage of studying at home is that one can study at their own pace, without having to catch up with other students who probably have different skills and abilities. Besides, a student can be undisturbed at

home whereas the school environment is noisier. Someone who studies at home can be calm, confident and relaxed, not worrying about competition against others and not getting stressed. Students who are shy and have difficulty talking to or socialising with other people are at ease when they study at home and can perform well.

On the other hand, studying at home can be boring, since there are no people of your age to talk to and joke with, which can also create a feeling of loneliness or confinement. Besides, studying at home cannot promote sociability or help someone overcome their shyness.

2 Someone's leisure activities contribute to the development of their character, as they are related to the person's skills and abilities. Someone who is keen on music, art or literature, for example, is most likely to develop into a sensitive person with a critical eye and an enquiring mind. Someone who devotes a lot of time to sports will inevitably become a health conscious, disciplined person. Someone interested in computers and electronic gadgets will tend to be practical and realistic. The way we spend our leisure time reflects our interests and affects our personality.
(Ss' own answers.)

3 Having a brother or sister plays a major role in the development of children from an early age. It is through interaction with their peers that young children learn how to communicate and develop their skills. This way they build their confidence and courage and slowly make their way into the world. Brothers and sisters share a very strong bond. It is usually our brother or sister that we can rely on for advice, help or support.
(Ss' own answers.)

Language Practice

(Suggested answer)

Meg appears to be very thoughtful and responsible, as she is willing to help the family after the girls' father loses his property. She is outgoing and sociable, wishing she could lead a way of life similar to the one her rich employers enjoy. This makes her appear a bit vain again, like in Chapter 2. However, this time too, she proves to be sensible and disciplined, trying not to feel envious of the King family's luxuries.

Jo is as thoughtful and responsible as Meg, offering to help the family after her father's misfortune. She is kind and sweet, looking after her aunt and forgiving the old lady's grumpiness. Above all, Jo appears to be intelligent, spending hours in Aunt March's library, looking through all her books. Also, she is very ambitious, wishing to achieve something significant one day.

Beth is very shy, which is the reason why she studies at home. She is a sensitive, sweet girl who cares about others. She helps Hannah with the housework and even takes care of her dolls. Beth is also musical, as she enjoys playing the piano, and never complains despite the family's difficulties.

Amy proves to be very artistic, as she spends hours drawing. In fact, it is the only thing that makes her happy. She even neglects her schoolwork, filling her books with drawings instead of sums. The only thing Amy seems to enjoy at school is her schoolmates' admiration for her, which makes her appear a bit vain or selfish. However, her flat nose and old clothes prevent her from being spoilt.

11 **Across**
1 LUXURIES
2 INSTRUMENTS
3 SUPPORT
4 TALENT
5 SLIPPERS
6 CLOSE

Down
7 CONSERVATORY
8 GRUMPY
9 SUMS
10 EMPLOYERS

What happens next?

Class discussion. Ss provide and justify their own answers.

Analysis

You may wish to help Ss analyse the meaning and the underlying implications of the following excerpts after the chapter has been read and the comprehension questions discussed.

- p.21: 'Meg and Amy were very close. Amy told Meg all her problems and worries. Jo and Beth had a similar relationship; Jo was the only person who really knew Beth's thoughts.' The March sisters appear to be very close, forming a very strong bond with each other. The younger ones, Amy and Beth, seem to look up to their older sisters, Meg and Jo. They confide in them and share their thoughts and troubles with them. Especially at this difficult time the family goes through, it is very important for the girls to know they have support and encouragement.

- p.22: 'She never realized that the old man opened his study door so that he could hear her music while he was working. She never knew that the books of music which she found on the piano were gifts for her.' Mr Lawrence is very discreet towards Beth. He doesn't want to embarrass her and acts without her noticing him. Due to her shy nature, Beth doesn't want to draw attention to herself, and Mr Laurence respects this. He silently enjoys her music and never tells her that the books of music are actually a present from him, which also shows how generous and selfless he is.

- p.22: 'Beth decided to make Mr. Laurence a pair of slippers to thank him for his generosity. She had been working on the slippers for several days and nights, and when they were ready, she placed them on Mr. Laurence's desk with a short note.' As if there is some silent agreement between Beth and Mr Laurence, she returns his generosity as discreetly, proving how kind and appreciative she is.

- p.23: "Dear Miss March,
I have had many pairs of slippers in my life, but I have never had any that suited me as well as yours. I hope you will allow me to

send you something which once belonged to my granddaughter, whose eyes were so like yours, and who I sadly lost. With all my thanks and best wishes,

James Laurence" Mr Laurence proves to be very kind-hearted once again when he gives Beth a piano as a present. Considering that the piano belonged to his dear granddaughter, it must be of great sentimental value to Mr Laurence. Yet, he doesn't hesitate to give it away, showing his kind nature.

Chapter 4 - Amy Gets into Trouble

Comprehension

1 b   2 a   3 b   4 c   5 b   6 a   7 c

What do you think?

A (Suggested answers)

1 The younger we are, the easier it is for us to get influenced by others. As children and teenagers, we lack wisdom and experience that come with age and maturity. What worries us most at this stage of our life is our need to be accepted by and integrate with our peers. This is the reason why we follow the latest fashions and even adopt attitudes that we would normally not accept. The people surrounding us, especially our friends, definitely influence the way we think and behave, and therefore affect our personality. For this reason, we must be very careful as to how we choose our friends. However, we must also learn to trust our judgment and not blindly accept what the others tell us.

2 Amy breaks the school rules when she brings limes with her, therefore she should be punished. However, Mr Davis proves to be very strict, as the punishment he imposes on

her is rather harsh. Even though he makes her throw her limes out of the window, he also hits her palm with his ruler and, finally, makes her stand at the front of the class until break-time. This makes Amy very embarrassed. Punishment is only acceptable as a means of discipline. Even in this case, however, it must be fair and reasonable, not a means of revenge and definitely not a way of abusing one's power.

3 It isn't always easy to forgive and forget people's cruelty or misdemeanours. When we feel that our dignity and pride are injured, we almost instinctively think of revenge. However, we shouldn't let anger prevail and make us vindictive. The ability to forgive shows magnanimity and strength of character. Besides, there is no point in perpetuating hatred. Instead, we should always find the courage to leave ill feeling behind and move on.

4 It is difficult for someone to change their character, especially when they have reached a certain age. The way we are brought up, including our family's guidance and the influence we get from our environment, plays a crucial role in the development of our personality. It isn't very easy for someone with set ideas and habits to change their character. What is not impossible, however, is for someone to try and work on their character flaws. We must always be receptive when it comes to self-improvement.

B **(Suggested answers)**

1 Amy's teacher proves to be very strict and inconsiderate. He humiliates her, as he embarrasses her in front of all her classmates. She is so ashamed that the only thing she can do when the bell rings is leave the classroom and run out of the school.

2 Although Amy has Meg's support when she asks her elder sisters to take her out with them, Jo does not consent. It seems that Meg, to whom Amy is closer, is more easy-going and relaxed whereas Jo, who is the oldest, tends to be bossy. Meg becomes so angry with Jo that she threatens her.

3   Jo realises that she shouldn't have treated Amy with contempt and she now feels guilty. If she hadn't ignored her little sister in the first place, perhaps Amy's life wouldn't have been in danger. Even now, though, Jo realises her mistake and admits she is bad-tempered. More importantly, she is willing to work on her flaw and try to become better.

Language Practice

1   (**Suggested answer**) Amy **breaks the rules** when she goes to school with a bag full of **limes**, and she is **severely punished** by her teacher. She is so **ashamed** that she never goes back to school but studies at home. However, she soon gets bored and asks her elder sisters to take her out with them. Jo **refuses** and the two girls end up having an argument. The next day, Jo decides to **go skating** with Laurie. Amy follows them but has an accident when she skates where the ice is **smooth**. Jo can't help **blaming** herself for ignoring her little sister and wishes she didn't **have** such **a bad temper**.

II 1 safe   4 solid   7 punishment
    2 rude   5 ashamed   8 wicked
    3 refuses   6 front

Analysis

You may wish to help Ss analyse the meaning and the underlying implications of the following excerpts after the chapter has been read and the comprehension questions discussed.

- p. 26: *"I wish I was rich like Laurie. I could pay off all my debts."* This is another occasion when lack of money in the March family is a problem. Amy feels in debt to the other girls at school and wishes she had money like Laurie. No matter how considerate and understanding the girls are, the practicalities of every day life are there to remind them of their predicament.
- p.26: *"The girls at school eat pickled limes. We're not supposed to have them at school, but all the girls bring them. They give them*

to their friends and swap them for pencils or paper dolls. I've had lots of limes from other girls. Now I have to give some back, but I don't have any money." Amy wants to be like the other girls at school so that she is accepted. Like most people at her age, she wants to integrate with her peers even if this means breaking the rules. Although she knows that she is not allowed to bring limes to school, she wishes she had the money to do so because this is what all the other girls do.

- p. 26: "How much money do you need?" As soon as Amy explains to Meg how things at school are, Meg immediately offers to help her. The two sisters have a very close relationship, and Meg, being older, acts like Amy's guardian angel.
- p. 28: "I'm sorry, but Laurie is taking us to the theater, and you're not invited." In contrast to Meg, who is soft and indulgent, Jo is very strict and steadfast. She doesn't allow herself to be sentimental but makes it clear that Amy cannot go out with them.
- p. 28: "If she goes, I'll stay here. Laurie only invited the two of us. It would be rude to take Amy as well." Jo shows complete lack of pity or sympathy for Amy. Even Meg's urging is not enough for Jo to change her mind. She insists on her decision not to take their sister out with them and even threatens to stay at home if Amy joins them.
- p. 29: "I burned it. You were horrible to me and you deserved it!" Jo's cold-heartedness causes Amy to take revenge. She wants to hurt her sister as she has hurt her, and the best way to do this is by destroying Jo's book. Amy knows how much Jo's stories mean to her, as she dreams of being a writer one day, and she doesn't hesitate to burn her sister's book, thinking it is the right punishment for Jo.
- p. 29: "I'll never forgive you, Amy. You're a wicked little girl!" Jo is so furious with Amy after what she has done to her that the tension between the two sisters builds up. If Jo was not willing to sympathise with Amy earlier, it is impossible that she will do it now, as her outburst of anger shows.

- p. 29: *"Jo promised to take me along the next time she went skating!"* Despite Amy's apology, Jo is taking pleasure in torturing her sister. Although she consented to take Amy skating with her, she doesn't keep her promise. As if doing it on purpose, she leaves with Laurie, making Amy even more distressed.
- p. 29: *"Go after them and find the right moment to make up with Jo."* Being close to her little sister, Meg sympathises with Amy and wants her to settle her dispute with Jo. She advises Amy to follow Jo so that they will make up again. She can't imagine that going skating will nearly cost Amy's life.

Chapter 5 - Meg Becomes a Lady

Comprehension

1 e   2 a   3 f   4 b   5 d   6 c

What do you think?

A **(Suggested answers)**
1. Getting informed about the latest trends in fashion is a good thing to do. It is always nice to keep up with our time and not be old-fashioned. However, we shouldn't buy something just because it is in fashion. We must always adjust the way we dress to our taste and personality and we must try and have our own personal style. Otherwise, we run the risk of having no personal identity, but looking exactly the same as numerous other people. Even worse, we run the risk of being something we are not and even making a spectacle of ourselves.
2. The Moffats are a wealthy, fashionable family who spend a lot of money on entertainment, so the Moffat sisters must be spoilt to some, if not to a large, extent. They don't have

to work at all but spend their time attending dinners, going to the theatre and shopping. Finding the right dress to wear and changing their hair each time seem to be their only worries. Their way of life makes them appear superficial, only caring about unimportant things and not paying attention to anything serious. Belle insists on lending Meg one of her dresses for the ball, helps her to curl her hair, puts jewellery on her and turns her into a different person. The Moffat sisters are all delighted at the result and don't realise that Meg is not herself anymore. Their whole attitude reveals a rather shallow character, as they treat people like dolls.

3 It is thanks to Laurie's straightforwardness that Meg realises how foolish she has been. Laurie actually brings her back to reality, making her see that she has renounced herself in the name of luxury and wealth. Although she is annoyed at first, thinking Laurie is rude, she later accepts the fact that she pretends to be something she isn't and wishes she could go back home. Laurie makes her see through herself and appreciate the real Meg; therefore he does the right thing when he tells her the truth about her appearance. As her friend, he must be sincere.

4 What makes a person admirable has nothing to do with clothes and appearance. It is character and personality that play a major role in our forming an impression of someone. Moral principles and values, honesty, respect and consideration for others are much more important than looks.

B **(Suggested answers)**

1 Laurie is shocked at Meg's new appearance. Having spent time with the March sisters, he has got to know each one and he is certainly not used to seeing Meg adopting such a style and manner. His words are a big disappointment to Meg, who was really proud of her appearance.

2 After Laurie's disappointing remarks, it is another guest's turn to make Meg lose heart. This time, her confidence is completely destroyed, as she realises that she has made a

spectacle of herself. She isn't being admired, as she thought, but mocked by people, since it is obvious to everyone that her appearance does not reflect her real self.
3 Despite Mrs March's pointing out that being poor but respected is much more important than being rich but undignified, Meg cannot help thinking of Belle's words. According to her rich friend, a poor girl is rather doomed to an unpromising future. As Meg is growing up, she is faced with the grim reality of their family's precarious position.

Language Practice

- attend dinners
- follow the latest fashions
- throw a party
- refuse sb's offer

- breathe a sigh of relief
- shake your head
- have a good time

1 breathes a sigh of relief
2 attend dinners
3 follow the latest fashions
4 shakes her head
5 throw a party
6 had a good time
7 refuse, offer

Analysis

You may wish to help Ss analyse the meaning and the underlying implications of the following excerpts after the chapter has been read and the comprehension questions discussed.

- p. 34 *"Meg would be so pretty if she had some nicer clothes. I must lend her a decent dress for the ball on Thursday."* Belle's words reveal the true nature of the Moffat family. The four sisters and their mother are only being polite to Meg regarding her appearance. In reality, they are embarrassed about Meg, who has a much lower status than the Moffat family, and want her to appear as respectable as possible in front of their rich guests.
- p. 35: *"Please, Laurie, don't tell my family how I looked tonight. Just say I looked nice and I had a good time."* On the one hand, Meg is embarrassed and doesn't want her family to know

about her unpleasant experience, at least not yet. On the other hand, she appears to be considerate, too. Perhaps, she doesn't want her mother and sisters to worry about her, thinking that she isn't having a good time with the Moffats. It is wiser to wait until she returns home and sees them.

- p. 35: *"I'm glad you think so, my dear. I was afraid home would not be good enough for you after all you have seen with the Moffats."* Mrs March is relieved to hear that Meg has missed home and is happy to be back. She knows that her daughter likes a fashionable life, and living with the Moffats must have been a great temptation for Meg to think twice before returning to her poor, simple life.

- p. 36: *"No, I behaved like a fool, too. I enjoyed being admired and having everyone look at me."* Despite the Moffats' insistence that Meg dress up like a doll, Meg does not fail to blame herself too for accepting the situation. She thought expensive clothes would make everyone admire her and she enjoyed being the centre of attention. Now she realises her behaviour was foolish, making her appear to be vain and shallow.

- p. 36: *"I want my daughters to be admired, but I want them to be loved and respected, too. There is nothing wrong with being poor if you are happy, honest and kind. It is better to be poor and happy than to be rich and have no self-respect."* Mrs March is giving her daughters a lesson on morality, distinguishing between right and wrong. There is nothing wrong with admiration as long as it is accompanied by respect. Wealth and extravagance are not always friends with respect, as they can lead someone to extremes and deprive them of self-respect. It is very important for someone to retain their dignity even if this means they have to lead a poor life.

- p. 36: *"Let time decide about that. For the moment, do your best to make this home a happy place. And remember; your father and I will always be here for you."* Mrs March is trying to dispel Megs fears. Her painful experience at the Moffat house taught her daughter an important lesson regarding self-respect. Still, Belle's words set Meg ill at ease. Her mother advises her to have faith in time and not prejudge the future. The best thing for her to do now is concentrate on the present, make the most of what she has and appreciate her family's love and support. This is very unusual and bold for a woman of that time to say, as women's futures then depended heavily on their choice of a well-off husband.

Chapter 6 - Secrets

Comprehension

1 d   2 b   3 f   4 a   5 c   6 g   7 e

What do you think?

A **(Suggested answers)**
1 Jo must feel very nervous before she visits the newspaper office. Although she hurries into town, she is very hesitant when she reaches the building. She goes in and out several times before she finally decides to walk back in. She must be afraid, as she doesn't know what to expect. Her desire to become a writer is so strong that she will be very disappointed if things don't go well. When Jo sees her story printed, however, her emotions are completely different. She must feel very satisfied with her achievement and proud of herself. She is independent now, able to support herself and also help her family, whom she has made very proud.
2 When Jo hears that Meg is in love with Mr Brooke, she gets upset. She feels she will lose her sister, and this keeps her in a bad mood for several days. On the one hand, it is obvious that Jo loves her sister deeply and doesn't want to be separated from her. On the other, her reaction is selfish. Instead of sharing Meg's happiness, she thinks

about herself. We should always encourage the ones we love in their choices and support their decisions when it comes to their happiness and well-being.

3 Laurie's reaction to hearing the news of Jo getting her stories printed by a newspaper shows how kind-hearted he is. He cries out happily and feels proud of her achievement. Similarly, Jo's family is extremely proud of her when they see her story in the newspaper and her name printed underneath. Mr Laurence also proves to be very kind-hearted when he offers to accompany Mrs March to Washington despite his old age. Mr Brooke appears to be equally considerate and caring when he undertakes the task of replacing Mr Laurence and escorting Mrs March on her journey. However, Jo is the one who proves to be really generous. She sells her hair in order to get money and help her sick father. Her sister Meg is at her side to comfort her and praise her for her kindness.

B (Suggested answers)

1 Laurie's enthusiasm when he finds out that Jo's first steps as a writer have been successful proves that he is a true friend. He doesn't get jealous of Jo; he isn't envious of her success. Instead, he congratulates her, crying out happily.

2 Jo makes the biggest sacrifice when she hears the bad news about her father's health. She doesn't hesitate to ruin her image by cutting her hair in order to save her father. Selling human hair to make wigs earned the owner a lot of money in the 19th century. This action proves Jo to be totally selfless. It shows how considerate and caring she is, sympathising with her father.

Language Practice

1 attic
2 editor
3 bundle
4 wigs
5 woods
6 tutor
7 independent
8 escort

A 2   B 4   C 1   D 3

What happens next?

Class discussion. Ss provide and justify their own answers.

Analysis

You may wish to help Ss analyse the meaning and the underlying implications of the following excerpts after the chapter has been read and the comprehension questions discussed.

- p. 37: *"That was quick, Jo! How many did you have pulled?"* Laurie cannot imagine that Jo has been to the newspaper office. Seeing her going into and out of the building, he assumes she has an appointment at the dentist's and is teasing her.

- p. 39: *"I saw Meg's glove in Mr. Brooke's pocket. Isn't that romantic?"* Laurie has been trying to arouse Jo's curiosity before revealing his big secret about Meg and Mr Brooke. He is being very light-hearted about it, seeing the whole situation as something pleasant and expects Jo to see it this way too.

- p. 39: *"I thought you'd be pleased."* Laurie is surprised to see Jo react the way she does to what he considers good news. The fact that Meg may be in love must make Jo happy. Instead, she looks very upset, thinking Mr Brooke will take Meg away from her.

- p. 40: *"My dear, where did you get this? I hope you didn't do anything foolish."* Mrs March cannot hide her concern when she sees Jo place a bundle of money in front of her. Ever since Mr March lost his property the whole family has been trying to make ends meet. Especially in this difficult period of their life, money is such a luxury that Mrs March cannot but wonder where Jo found so much money.

- p. 41: *"Oh, Jo, how could you! You don't look like you any more!"* Although everyone stares in surprise when they see Jo's different hairstyle, Meg is the only one who appears to be shocked. The vain side of Meg's character makes her pay so much attention to appearance that it is hard for her to accept Jo's change. She appears to be inconsiderate, not realising her words may hurt her sister.

- p. 41: *"My head feels nice and cool. I'm sure it will do my brains good to have more air!"* Despite Meg's insensitivity, Jo is brave enough to remain calm and even joke about the situation. She doesn't want her family to feel bad about her, thinking she is sad or miserable, and she convinces them of the contrary.
- p. 41: *"No, you don't. You look beautiful, and you did a very kind thing. Don't worry. I'll make your hair curl for you."* Meg now sympathises with Jo and tries to make her feel better. She praises her for her kind-heartedness and offers to make her hair curly so that she doesn't feel ugly.

Chapter 7 - Beth's Kindness

Comprehension

1 keep busy
2 gets better
3 does housework
4 holding a bottle of medicine
5 Beth is going to have scarlet fever
6 not to tell their mother anything about Beth
7 her sisters' attitude changes
8 is glad

What do you think?

A **(Suggested answers)**
   1 Seeing Beth suffering in pain, Meg and Jo come to a sudden realisation. Meg is no longer obsessed with wealth, as she realises she has things that money can't buy: love, peace and health. As for Jo, she realises that talent, wealth or beauty are not as important as caring for others. It is in

difficult times that we appreciate the things we have. It is always when we are in danger of losing things that we understand how valuable they are. Under normal circumstances, we tend to take things for granted, often underestimating their importance and failing to treasure them.
2 Unity is very important in times of crisis. It is through collective action that people can work out a solution to a problem and overcome a difficult situation. Regardless of the outcome, the feeling of togetherness makes people strong and hopeful. Beth's family proves to be very united, as all members are attached to each other. The girls try not to lose heart when their mother leaves for Washington. They keep busy and don't neglect to write a hopeful letter to their parents every day. When Beth becomes ill, she has her sisters' care and support. Even though the girls temporarily hide the truth about Beth's health from their mother, they change their mind when things change for the worse. They feel the need to be united as a family and they call Mother back.

B **(Suggested answers)**
1 Jo and Beth share a special bond, as Jo is the one who Beth confides in. Therefore, it comes as no surprise that Jo is terribly worried when she hears the news about Beth's illness. She wants to keep Beth safe and immediately gets involved in the situation, making her little sister feel she is not alone.
2 Hannah appears to be very considerate towards Mrs March, as she doesn't want to burden her with another worry. She knows the girls' mother is already concerned about Mr March, and feels that finding out about Beth's illness would only agitate her more. Thinking that Beth will soon recover, Hannah decides to protect Mrs March from further anxiety.

Language Practice

H	E	A	L	T	H	A	E
O	P	O	I	U	C	T	R
S	Y	M	P	T	O	M	S
P	R	E	X	N	L	E	O
I	F	D	Z	P	D	I	R
T	T	I	O	K	O	L	E
A	G	C	R	C	R	F	E
L	H	I	E	P	A	I	N
E	J	N	E	L	A	O	E
D	F	E	V	E	R	D	R

1. sore
2. hospital
3. fever
4. cold
5. pain
6. symptoms
7. health
8. medicine

Analysis

You may wish to help Ss analyse the meaning and the underlying implications of the following excerpts after the chapter has been read and the comprehension questions discussed.

- p. 45: *"I looked in Mother's medical book. I've got a headache and a sore throat, and these are the symptoms. I took some medicine and I think I'll be fine."* Although Beth is very worried that she may be sick, she tries not to show it. She doesn't want Jo to be worried too, and doesn't sound emotional at all. Instead, she takes a matter-of-fact tone and appears to be confident that she will be fine.

- p. 45: *"You've been with the baby and with the other children who have the fever. I'm afraid you are going to have it, Beth. Oh, I wish Mother was at home."* Despite Beth's effort to appear calm, Jo cannot help worrying about her little sister. She is realistic, and cannot ignore the facts. Beth is most likely going to be ill and there is nothing they can do about it. Jo probably feels helpless and, in her despair, she wishes their mother was there with them.

- p. 45: *"We must keep Amy away. She hasn't had scarlet fever and I don't want her to catch it."* Beth keeps trying to appear calm.

Getting emotional and lamenting her misfortune would not be of any help. Instead, she sounds very reasonable and considerate as well, wanting to protect Amy from getting ill.

- p. 46: *'But poor Beth became more and more ill. She was very patient and she did not complain, but it was clear that she was in a lot of pain. Her hands moved on the bed covers as if she was playing an invisible piano and she sang in a quiet, broken voice.'* Beth has always been kind and sweet. She thinks of the people around her and never complains. She doesn't want to be a burden or impose herself on anyone, even at this difficult time she is going through. She tolerates her agony without saying a word. Her only comfort is her imaginary piano.

- p. 47: *"I've sent for Mother. I'm glad Father is better. Now Mother won't feel so bad about leaving him. But what about Beth? I love her so much and I can't lose her! I can't! Oh, I wish Mother were here now!"* Jo is getting really desperate to help Beth. She can't stand the idea of losing her but there is nothing she can do, and this must make her feel frustrated. Her mother's absence cannot but make things worse. Jo feels insecure, having no one to turn to for comfort and support. She therefore sends for Mother, who won't feel guilty about leaving her husband, as his health is improving.

- p. 47: *"Oh, Laurie! I'm so glad! Thank you!"* Jo sounds relieved. Her anxiety will soon come to an end, as Laurie has already sent for Mrs March. He proves to be very caring and considerate, trying to do the best he can to help.

Chapter 8 - Mrs March Returns

Comprehension

1 When Jo sees that Beth's face looks different, she thinks her sister has died.
2 The first thing Beth sees when she wakes up is her mother's face.
3 Mrs March's journey home has been delayed by a storm.
4 During her stay at Aunt March's, Amy realises she is very selfish.
5 Jo is surprised by her mother's friendly attitude towards Mr Brooke.
6 Mrs March thinks Meg is too young to get married.
7 Jo worries that John will take Meg away.

What do you think?

A **(Suggested answers)**
1 The last few days had been very difficult for Mrs March. When she was informed about her husband's poor health, she had to leave for Washington immediately to be at his side. The fact that she found him dangerously ill must have caused her great anxiety and pain. No sooner had she been relieved to see Mr March get better than she was informed about Meg's bad condition. This means she had to experience the same situation twice, which must have been really stressful for her. Her delayed journey home must have also increased her tension, so when she arrived she was probably emotionally and psychologically exhausted.
2 Most people tend to associate money with happiness, missing out on more important things in life. Undoubtedly, money is important for someone to improve their living conditions but it is not indispensable for someone's well-being. No matter how rich someone is, if they have no one to share their life with they can't be happy. Being loved and cared for is what happiness is about. Money cannot make up for a lack of these things.

3 Growing up signifies a new stage in someone's life. It is the moment when a young person starts to have worries and things to take care of, the time when life becomes a bit more complicated as childhood gives way to adulthood. This is why Jo seems to be at a loss. Her sister's prospect of marriage makes her realise that they are no longer children and, therefore, will have more responsibilities to undertake. (Ss' own answers.)

B **(Suggested answers)**

1 Jo and Meg are not the only ones who make an important realisation about themselves during Beth's illness. Amy too comes to an important conclusion after all the time she has spent away from home. Her stay with Aunt March has made her more responsible and hardworking. She has learnt to help others and not only care about herself. She now realises how selfish she has been and is willing to become better.

2 Jo cannot hide her disappointment at Mr Brooke's interest in Meg. She can't accept the fact that he will take her away from the rest of the family by marrying her, and she dreads the thought of Meg falling in love with him. She isn't prepared yet to move on to the next stage in her life. She wants to remain a child and enjoy her time with her sisters.

Language Practice

1 c   2 h   3 a   4 e   5 d   6 b   7 f   8 g

1 will fall in love   4 reaching   7 keep, safe
2 whispers   5 sits, lap   8 get engaged
3 afford   6 waits for

What happens next?

Class discussion. Ss provide and justify their own answers.

> Analysis

You may wish to help Ss analyse the meaning and the underlying implications of the following excerpts after the chapter has been read and the comprehension questions discussed.

- p. 48: *"Goodbye, my dear Beth. Goodbye."* Beth's sudden change deceives Jo into believing her little sister has died. Beth is no longer flushed with fever and doesn't seem to be in pain. On the contrary, she looks very pale and serene. Jo, however, has been prepared for the worst and interprets Beth's condition as a bad sign.
- p. 48: *"Oh, my goodness! The fever has gone! She's going to live!"* Hannah cannot believe Beth's health has improved. As the girl has taken a turn for the worse all these days, this sudden development catches everyone unaware. Hannah is the first to notice and she cannot hide her astonishment.
- p. 49: *"Who is John?"* Jo is very surprised to hear her mother call Mr Brooke by his first name. She is completely unaware of the intimacy between him and her parents. This realisation now comes as a shock to her, as she sees that her chances of keeping Meg in the family are becoming slighter.
- p. 49: *"Mr. Brooke. I call him John now, because he has been like a son to your father and me. He told us that he has fallen in love with Meg, and wants to marry her. But he's sensible, too, and wants to earn enough to buy a nice house before he asks her. He is an excellent young man and I hope Meg will love him, but I don't want her to get engaged yet. She is still too young."* It seems that Mrs March has grown very fond of Mr Brooke. He undertook the task of accompanying her to Washington to see her sick husband, and it seems that the three of them developed a close friendship. Mr Brooke proves to be so trustworthy that Mr and Mrs March see him as their son. He seems like a promising young man, who has a real interest in Meg.
- p. 51: *"I don't want you to say anything to Meg about this yet. When John comes back, we will see how Meg feels about him."* Mrs March doesn't want to rush things between Mr Brooke

and Meg. Therefore, it would serve no purpose for Jo to tell Meg about Mr Brooke's interest in her. Meg is too young to marry, anyway, so it would be better if John came back from Washington first and everything took its course.

- p. 51: *"I understand how you feel, dear. I want to keep my girls for as long as I can. But Meg is only seventeen and John cannot afford a house yet. So, your father and I have agreed that we won't let her get married until she is twenty. If she and John love one another, they can wait. It will be a good test of their love."* Mrs March sounds reassuring. She can understand Jo's misery, since losing a sister is as hard as losing a daughter. The fact that Meg is not allowed to marry until twenty is a kind of relief for the moment but it is also a test of the couple's love. If John and Meg really love one another, they will wait.

- p. 51: *"I hoped that Meg would marry Laurie. He's rich and good and he wouldn't take her away from me. Don't you want Meg to marry a rich man?"* Jo tries to come up with a way of keeping her sister close to her. She suggests that Meg marry Laurie, who is rich and good. She can't understand why her mother wouldn't want Meg to marry someone who not only has money but also won't take her away from her family. In her attempt to stay together with Meg, Jo rationalises everything.

Chapter 9 - Love Letters

Comprehension

1 daydreaming
2 annoyed
3 handwriting
4 alarmed
5 love letter
6 joke
7 bad mood
8 gives an apology

> **What do you think?**

A (**Suggested answers**)
1 Everyone has their own distinct sense of humour, which means that the way they react to jokes is very personal. What one sees as a joke does not necessarily have the same effect on someone else. Whether someone is amused or offended by a joke depends on their character and personal experiences as well as their cultural and religious background. Therefore, we have to think twice before playing a joke on someone.
2 When Mrs March hears that Meg replied to Mr Brooke's love letter she becomes alarmed. Soon after, when she finds out what her daughter's intentions are, her peace of mind is restored. Mrs March is very close to her children, guiding them without restricting their freedom. However, it is only natural that as a parent she worries about her daughters' well-being. Meg responding to Mr Brooke's feelings would probably be a rash action. Getting married at such a young age is not a wise thing to do, and when Meg proves sensible enough to politely turn down Mr Brooke's proposal, her mother cannot but be relieved.
3 When people face a difficult situation, it is common practice for them to run away and avoid dealing with it or taking responsibility. This is obviously not the best course of action for someone to take, as it only provides a temporary solution to a problem which, if not dealt with, will arise again in the future. In Laurie's case, he seems to want to take revenge on his grandfather for being so unforgiving, but this is not the charitable thing to do. It is always better to be brave enough to confront our problems and not ignore them, prolonging an unpleasant situation.
4 When Laurie suggests that Jo and he go to Washington, Jo gets tempted to run away with him. The idea of escaping reality for a while and having fun seems very appealing

to her. However, the thought of separating from her mother and sisters immediately makes her change her mind. Family is very important to Jo. She wouldn't sacrifice it for her personal pleasure. She is so close to her family that she would definitely miss them, and besides she doesn't wish to make them worry about her.
(Ss' own answers.)

B (**Suggested answers**)
1 Mrs March sounds panicky. She doesn't know if she can trust Meg's judgement, and the thought that her daughter might have behaved as rashly as to reply to Mr Brooke and encourage him makes her nervous.
2 Laurie is so excited at the idea of becoming independent that he acts almost childishly. He longs to go away without thinking about the possible implications of his decision. He wants Jo to go with him, too, trying to convince her that it will be safe and fun. In contrast to her, he appears to be very thoughtless and inconsiderate.

Language Practice

1 different
2 share
3 writing
4 relieved
5 playing
6 embarrass
7 stubborn

Guess the meaning

(**Suggested answers**)
event = sth that takes place
guest = a person invited somewhere
spoil = destroy
mumble = speak in an unclear way
brave = not afraid

> **Analysis**

You may wish to help Ss analyse the meaning and the underlying implications of the following excerpts after the chapter has been read and the comprehension questions discussed.

- p. 53: *"Meg has all the symptoms of being in love, Mother. She doesn't sleep, she doesn't eat, and she sits in corners, daydreaming. Whenever someone mentions Mr. Brooke's name, Meg's face turns red. What are we going to do?"* Although everyone is careful to keep Mr Brooke's love for Meg a secret, Jo cannot help noticing the change in her sister's behaviour. Everything points to the fact that she is in love. Jo feels they must do something about it and immediately asks Mother's advice.

- p.53: *"We must wait until your father comes home. Until then, we must be kind and patient with Meg."* Although the girls' father is absent, fighting in the war, he is still considered the head of the family, the one to take decisions about important matters. Mrs March appears to acknowledge her husband's role in the family. Now that he is away, she has undertaken the difficult task of also being a father to the girls. This, however, does not make her disregard him.

- p. 54 *"No! I'd never do something like this! In any case, I would have written a much better note than this one! Mr. Brooke would never have written something like this either!"* Jo is defending herself against her mother's and Meg's accusations. For one thing, she would never play a trick on Meg. For another, she would have written a much better note. Being a writer, Jo criticises the note Meg has received as poorly written, and appears a bit snobbish.

- p. 54 *"I told him that I was too young to marry and that he should speak to Father. I told him I was grateful for his kindness, but that I could only be his friend for now."* Meg proves to be sensible enough to give Mr Brooke the right answer and calm her mother's fears. In a polite but firm way, she declines his proposal and offers him her friendship. She also doesn't fail to refer to her father as the one Mr Brooke should speak to and ask permission from, showing respect to him like her mother did earlier.

- p.54: *"Yes, but he told me that he had never sent me a love letter! He said it must have been Jo playing a joke!"* Meg is shocked to receive Mr Brooke's reply to her note to him. She must now feel doubly embarrassed, as he confirms her initial suspicion that he has never sent her a love letter.
- p.56: *"Mr. Brooke doesn't know anything about the joke, and I'll never tell him. I'm very sorry, Meg. I hope you'll forgive me."* Laurie's joke causes him to suffer embarrassment and humiliation. It was a very thoughtless act, touching a sensitive issue, almost ridiculing a person and incriminating another. When he realises the seriousness of his action, he cannot but be penitent and apologetic, offering Meg great relief.
- p. 57: *"My grandfather got furious and shouted at me because I wouldn't tell him why I had gone to your house. I didn't want to tell him because I didn't want to embarrass Meg. He should trust me! I'm not a baby. I'm going to Washington to see Mr. Brooke and I'm not telling my grandfather where I'm going! When he misses me, he'll feel sorry."* His grandfather's distrust towards him makes Laurie feel disappointed. He wants to be treated like an adult, not like a baby, and he feels offended. Driven by anger, he wants to take revenge in a way. He is planning to leave without telling Mr Laurence so that he can prove he is old enough to take care of himself. Laurie's behaviour, however, makes him appear immature. Instead of confronting his grandfather, he chooses to run away.
- p. 57: *"Maybe, but you shouldn't worry him."* Being able to control her anger now, Jo tries to make Laurie calm down and act sensibly. What he intends to do is pointless, as it will only distress his grandfather greatly.

Chapter 10 - Meg's Decision

Comprehension

Father	2	Aunt March	3
Laurie	6	Beth	5
Jo	8	Amy	7
Meg	1	Mr Brooke	4

What do you think?

A (Suggested answers)

1 Laurie's actions throughout the story prove him to be a very good friend, sharing in everyone's happiness and sympathising with them in difficult times. Now, as the March family is about to celebrate Christmas, he helps Jo prepare a surprise for Beth. He even helps Jo carry Beth, who has been ill in bed for days. Laurie is the one who announces, in a way, Mr March's arrival, preparing his wife and daughters for a big surprise and getting as excited as they are. He is also the one who comforts Jo and tries to alleviate her sorrow, offering to be there for her when Meg leaves the family.

2 Aunt March seems to be very authoritative. She expects Meg to obey her, regardless of her own wishes. She sounds very cruel, renouncing love in the name of interest. She disapproves of Mr Brooke's marriage proposal to Meg, as she thinks Meg should marry a rich man and help her family. She even threatens Meg that she will inherit nothing from her if she doesn't listen to her. Aunt March is very old-fashioned and conservative. She expects Meg to sacrifice her personal happiness and conform to a stereotypical pattern of behaviour.

3 Class discussion. Ss provide and justify their own answers.

B (Suggested answers)
1 Mr March is very kind and thoughtful. He has just come back from the war and reunited with his family after a long time, and really appreciates the effort they have all made this year. He doesn't fail to acknowledge their improvement and praise them, proving to be very considerate and caring.
2 Aunt March is trying to persuade Meg that she is making a big mistake. There is no point in marrying out of love and living in poverty. Money is more important than romance, and it won't be long before she realises that and regrets her decision. Aunt March is also trying to make Meg feel guilty, as she shouldn't only think about herself but her family too. A prosperous marriage would benefit them as well.

Language Practice

Across
1 joyful
2 brighten
3 event
4 approach

Down
5 delicious
6 cottage
7 improve
8 unpleasant

What's the moral?

(Suggested answer)
Little Women deals with a number of issues which are of great importance even today. Overall, the prevalent notion in the story is that perseverance in hard work always gets rewarded, sometimes against the odds. Setting a goal and dedicating ourselves to its achievement gives us strength and courage through a difficult period. This is a reward in itself regardless of the outcome. Having something to hope for and to expect is what keeps us going.

Culture Corner

(Suggested answer)

The American Civil War (1861-1865) took place in the United States of America, when eleven slave states in the south (the Confederacy) fought against the federal government in the north supported by all free states (the Union). In the slave states, slavery of African Americans was legal whereas in the free states slavery was prohibited. In 1860, Abraham Lincoln, about to become President of the United States, led a political campaign against the expansion of slavery. This encouraged seven Southern slave states to declare their separation from the United States, which the government considered rebellion. In April 1861, the Confederate forces attacked the Union and were soon joined by another four Southern slave states. It wasn't long before the abolition of slavery in the South became the main goal of the war, which was finally achieved. President Lincoln played a leading role in giving all former slaves the right to become US citizens protected by the law. Not only did he guarantee the permanent abolition of slavery but he also preserved and strengthened the Union, successfully leading the country through this great crisis. Moreover, he blocked other countries from entering the war and thus eliminated a European threat.

Right from the beginning of the war, the North had a significant advantage over the South in terms of population and industrial strength; Lincoln managed to keep the border states, slave states bordering a free state, committed to the Union. Also, the North's industrialised economy, which grew even more during the war, facilitated the production of weapons and transportation. These were the crucial factors that determined the South's defeat. Regardless of the inequalities between the two opposing sides, the American Civil War was the deadliest war in American history. The reconstruction era that followed the end of the war influenced the country decisively, helping it become a united superpower.

> Analysis

You may wish to help Ss analyse the meaning and the underlying implications of the following excerpts after the chapter has been read and the comprehension questions discussed.

- p. 59: *"I remember when this hand was white and smooth, and you wanted to keep it that way. It was very pretty then, but I prefer it like this. It shows that you have worked hard for your family."* Mr March is praising Meg, acknowledging the fact that during his absence she became a hard-working, responsible person. Her hands might not be as delicate now but they show how hard she has worked for her family, which is far more important.

- p. 59: *"Despite your short hair, you are not the boyish Jo who I left a year or so ago. You are a young lady now. I shall miss my wild girl, but I love the strong, helpful and kind girl who has replaced her."* It is Jo's turn now to receive her father's words of praise. She has changed a lot too during this year. She does not behave like a boy now, despite her boyish haircut. Her wildness has given way to kindness and consideration.

- p. 59: *"You're safe now, my Beth, and I'll keep you that way."* Mr March is particularly tender to Beth. She is the most sensitive of the four sisters, and the life-threatening episode with her health has made her even more fragile. Her father is reassuring and protective, making her feel safe.

- p. 62: *"Amy helped her mother all afternoon and served everyone at dinner. She does not look in mirrors any more and I have not heard her complain about anything. I think Amy has learnt to think of other people instead of herself. I am very proud of her."* The passage of time does not leave Amy unaffected, either. She has become more sensitive to other people's needs and doesn't only think of herself now. She has become a better person, as she is more tolerant and considerate now, and her father has every reason to be proud of her.

- p. 62: *"Please go away and don't think of me!"* Meg overcomes her embarrassment and verbally attacks Mr Brooke, who must be shocked at her sudden change of behaviour. Their private discussion, which was in a way forced upon Meg, seems to have put Meg in a state of agitation. Perhaps she feels forced to give an answer without being ready to do so. She might even feel flattered to have attracted a man's attention, realising she is not a little girl anymore, and this makes her act like a grown-up person.
- p. 63: *"Mother and Father don't think so. They like John. He may be poor, but he is good and kind. I am lucky to have his love."* Meg is defending John against Aunt March's severe criticism. To Meg, it is not money but character that counts, and John has proved that he has an impeccable character. The fact that Meg's parents approve of him is Meg's strongest argument against her aunt's biased views.
- p. 63: *"Thank you for defending me. Now I know you care for me."* It is only when Meg supports John that he can be sure of her feelings for him. Until now she has been too embarrassed to express herself in words. After the incident with Aunt March, however, Meg finds the bravery she has lacked so far to admit her feelings to herself.
- p. 63: *"It will never be the same again. I've lost my dearest friend."* Even now that the March family is reunited, rejoicing at the news of Meg's marriage, Jo remains inconsolable. Her sister's happiness is not enough to make up for her own misery.
- p. 63: *"Everyone is so happy. I don't think life could get any better for them."* Jo cannot but cheer up a little when she sees everyone

Project A

A Review

1 A, B, C, E, F, G, I

2 c) semi-formal

3 The review is divided into four paragraphs.
   (suggested paragraph headings):
   1st par.: Introduction
   2nd par.: Brief plot outline
   3rd par.: General comments
   4th par.: Recommendations

4

Background	Main points of the plot	General comments	Recommendations
• The book/ novel was written by ... • The story is set in ... • It is a thriller/ love story/ science fiction novel ... • (*David Copperfield*) is a story describing ...	• The plot has an unexpected twist. • The plot is rather predictable/ absolutely fascinating ... • It has a happy/ tragic/ dramatic ending. • The story begins when ...	• The book is poorly/ badly written ... • It is a boring/ entertaining read ... • All the characters are well portrayed. • This is a beautifully written book ...	• If you like (science fiction), this book is for you. • I wouldn't recommend it because ... • You won't be able to put this book down. • I strongly recommend this book (to) ...

5 (Suggested answer)

LITTLE WOMEN

Little Women, by Louisa May Alcott, is the story of four girls who grow into young women. It is set during the American Civil War and focuses on the girls' and their mother's struggle against poverty and everyday hardships while their father is away fighting in the war.

The story begins when the March sisters all brood over the unattractive prospect of Christmas due to lack of money. The novel guides the reader through a series of events in which the girls learn to change their attitude and appreciate what they have. They change to self-sufficient and responsible young ladies, learning valuable lessons from each one of their everyday experiences.

Little Women is an entertaining read, presenting us with four different types of girls who were all apparently inspired by the writer's actual family.

If you like didactic novels, this book is for you. Its detailed study of moral standards in 19th century America provides a striking contrast to modern ethics. At the same time, the portrayal of the transition from childhood to adulthood still touches the reader.

Project B

My Favourite Character

1 (Suggested answers)

1 My favourite character is Jo.
2 Jo does not look like a typical girl of her era, as she behaves more like a tomboy and not like a young lady. She doesn't care about her appearance much and doesn't look after her clothes. She must be a bit bulky or large, since her hand doesn't fit well in Meg's glove. She wears her long thick hair in a plait until she has it cut short, appearing even less feminine.
3 Jo appears to be a vigorous girl who dares to go after her dreams and fulfil her ambitions. She is intelligent and very determined, managing to get through difficulties and maintain her morale. She is very kind and considerate, thinking of others and trying to keep her family united. She can be stubborn and bossy at times because of her hot temper but she realises her faults and weaknesses and tries to become better. She prefers hanging around with boys but feels too young to get emotionally involved with any of them.
4 Jo is the second oldest of the four sisters and Beth's confidante. She is involved in almost every major event in the story and her involvement affects the plot significantly. She is witness to her family's misadventures and the changes they all undergo, trying to alleviate crisis and keep the family together. She struggles to prolong the carefree days of childhood and laments the loss of innocence as her sisters and she are forced to grow up abruptly.
5 The main reason why Jo is my favourite character is that she does not compromise but is ready to put up a fight when circumstances call for it. She is a girl of action, bold enough to take risks. Contrary to the social standards of her time that do not allow for women's independence but keep them confined at home, Jo breaks free from convention and sets out to be a writer. She is also very thoughtful and caring; she sacrifices

her hair to save her father, can't stand the thought of losing Beth, when the latter gets ill, and does not want to be separated from Meg when she marries. Jo proves to be a good friend, keeping Laurie company when he is ill and reconciling him with his grandfather. Lastly, she works hard to be able to control her temper and not hurt the people around her.

6 *"I'll try to be a little woman and stop being rough and wild."* (p.9) Jo was sitting on her favorite sofa by the sunny window in the attic, eating an apple and reading a book. / *"Your dress is fine, but mine has a burn and a tear in the back."* / *"My gloves are ruined, Meg. I spilled lemonade on them. Never mind. I'll hold them in my hand and I won't dance. No! We can each wear one good glove and carry a stained one."* (p.14)

Jo did not care for the girlish gossip. She longed to join the boys on the other side of the room and talk about boyish things, but she knew Meg would not approve. / Remembering Meg's lectures to her about not winking, holding her shoulders straight, not shaking hands – as it wasn't ladylike – and how Meg would raise her eyebrows if Jo was doing something wrong, Jo realized that she would never learn all of the proper ways of being a lady. / Jo saw a boy walking towards her to invite her to dance. Feeling suddenly shy, she slipped behind a curtain into a hidden corner of the room. / *"I'm not Miss March. I'm just Jo."* (p.16)

What Jo was really fond of, however, was Aunt March's library. She spent many happy hours in that dim, dusty room, looking through the books while Aunt March was asleep. Devouring every single line or verse, Jo's ambition was to achieve something important one day. (p.20)

Jo felt lucky to have three sisters to talk to, and she felt sorry for Laurie, who had no brothers at all. In the days after New Year, Laurie had been ill with a bad cold, so one snowy afternoon Jo decided to visit him and read to him to cheer him up a little. (p.21) Jo was very straightforward. *"I'm sorry, but Laurie is taking us to the theater, and you're not invited."* / Jo insisted. *"If she goes, I'll stay here. Laurie invited the two of us. It would be rude to take Amy as well."* (p.28)

Jo liked to think of herself as a writer, and had spent many hours writing these stories. / "I'll never forgive you, Amy. You're a wicked little girl!" / Jo saw her sister, but she was still so angry with her that she turned her back and skated away from her. (p.29)
When Amy was sleeping by the fire, Jo watched her with sadness and love in her eyes. / Jo, however, could not help blaming herself. "But if she had died, it would have been my fault. I wish I didn't have such a bad temper. How can I stop myself from getting so angry?" (p.30)
"Jo wanted me to come. She wanted to know how you looked." (p.34)
Meg smiled but, after Beth and Amy had gone to bed, she told Jo and Mother all about the ball. (p.35)
Jo began to spend her time in the attic, where she wrote busily, filling sheet after sheet of paper. (p.37)
"All right. I've given two stories to the newspaper. The editor is going to tell me if he will print them next week." / "Of course I'm not pleased. I don't want anyone to take Meg away from me." / The best news of all was that the newspaper's editor wanted Jo to write more stories and promised to pay her for them. Jo was delighted. To be independent and to make the people she loved proud of her were her two dearest wishes. (p.39)
"I want you to use this money to make Father well and bring him home, Mother." (p.40)
"My head feels nice and cool. I'm sure it will do my brains good to have more air!" / "I'm not sorry. I'd do it again tomorrow to help Father or any of you. It's just that I look so ugly now!" (p.41)
Jo hugged Beth and cried out. "No, you won't! I can't let you be ill. What shall we do?" (p.45)
Jo finally understood that caring for others was more important than talent, wealth or beauty. / Meg and Jo heard the doctor's words. Meg fell into a chair but Jo ran from the house to send a telegram to Mrs. March. (p.46)

"I've sent for Mother. I'm glad Father is better. Now Mother won't feel so bad about leaving him. But what about Beth? I love her so much and I can't lose her! I can't! Oh, I wish Mother were here now!" (p.47)
"Oh! It's worse than I imagined. I wish I could marry Meg myself, and keep her safe in the family." / "She'll fall in love with him, and that will be the end of our happy times together." / "I hoped that Meg would marry Laurie. He's rich and good and he wouldn't take her away from me. Don't you want Meg to marry a rich man?" / "Oh, Mother, I wish we didn't have to grow up." (p.51)
"Meg has all the symptoms of being in love, Mother. She doesn't sleep, she doesn't eat, and she sits in corners, daydreaming. Whenever someone mentions Mr. Brooke's name, Meg's face turns red. What are we going to do?" (p.53)
"No! I'd never do something like this! In any case, I would have written a much better note than this one! Mr. Brooke would never have written something like this either!" / "I don't believe that Mr. Brooke wrote either of these notes. I think Laurie wrote both and kept yours. I'm going to fetch that horrible little boy right now!" (p.54)
Seeing his sorry face, Meg forgave him immediately, but Jo was still very angry with him. She refused to smile at him, although she could tell that this hurt him a lot. (p.56)
"Don't be silly, Laurie. If I talk to your grandfather and ask him to apologize for getting so angry with you, will you forget about running away?" (p.57)

Name of Character
Jo March

Part in the story
She comes up with ways of dealing with difficulties and tries to keep the family united.

Personality
Jo is a fighter and a risk-taker; she is determined and courageous; she is considerate towards others despite her hot temper.

My feelings towards the character
I admire Jo for her bravery, strength of character and sense of independence. She isn't afraid to pursue her dream of becoming a writer and doesn't give up until she fulfils it.

2 (Suggested answer)

My favourite character in *Little Women* is Jo. As well as being a tomboy with a sense of independence rare in women of her time, she has a loving and affectionate nature.

Jo's efforts to keep the family united while Mr March is away are clearly displayed when she cuts off her hair to help support the family financially. She is also a great problem solver, settling the difficulty of the gloves she and Meg are to wear at the New Year's Eve ball and smoothing out the argument between Laurie and his grandfather.

Jo shows great courage and determination in her ambition to become a writer. This was difficult for women in the 19th century. Jo is prepared to take risks and fight for recognition, as when she takes her stories to the newspaper in great secrecy to avoid being seen. Characterised by her hot temper, this does not stop Jo being considerate towards others. She takes care of both Beth and Laurie when they are ill.

Finally, it is Jo's bravery and determination to become a writer, like Louisa May Alcott herself, which impresses me most.

✓ Final Check A

Listening

A. Listen to the recording, then fill in the gaps with one word.

Meg tried to refuse Belle's offer, but Belle 1) .... that she would make Meg into a true beauty. So, on Thursday evening, Belle and her 2) .... curled Meg's hair, 3) .... her dress very tightly and put silver jewelry on her. When Meg was finally 4) ...., the Moffat sisters were all delighted at how beautiful she looked, and they 5) .... her into the drawing room. Everyone 6) .... as Meg walked into the room. They all wanted to know who the beautiful young lady was. Meg felt very flattered by all the 7) .... She played with her fan and 8) .... and laughed with a young gentleman who tried to 9) .... her. Suddenly, she saw Laurie on the other 10) .... of the room and went to greet him.

10x2=20

20

Story

B. Put the following events in the correct chronological order.

1 ... a The girls take their breakfast to the Hummel family.
2 ... b Meg and Jo go to the New Year's Eve party.
3 ... c The girls find books under their pillows from Mother.
4 ... d The girls go to visit Laurie at his house.
5 ... e Jo meets Laurie behind the curtain.

5x3=15

15

C. Explain what you think was meant by the following.

1 Chapter 1, p. 13: "Is this from Father Christmas?"
   ....

2 Chapter 2, p. 41: "I'm not sorry. I'd do it again tomorrow to help Father or any of you. It's just that I look so ugly now!"
   ....

3 Chapter 9, p. 53: "It can't be from Mr. Brooke. It must be a trick. You wrote it, Jo, and that bad boy helped you. How could you be so unkind?"
   ....

3x10=30

30

New Words

D. Fill in the gaps with a word from the box.

| ashamed   elegant   library   confirmed   hospitable |

1 The doctor .... that Beth had scarlet fever.
2 Jo was very fond of Aunt March's ....
3 After playing a joke on Meg, Laurie felt ....
4 Mr Laurence proved to be very ....
5 When Meg and Jo dressed up for Mrs Gardiner's ball, they looked very ....

5x3=15

15

E. Fill in the gaps with the correct form of the words in capitals.

1 Beth made Mr Laurence a pair of slippers to thank him for his .... **GENEROUS**
2 Jo and Aunt March .... argued. **OCCASION**
3 Mr Laurence finally gave an .... to Laurie. **APOLOGISE**
4 Meg tried not to be .... of her rich employers' luxuries. **ENVY**
5 When Meg turned seventeen, she didn't care for .... games. **CHILD**

5x4=20

20

Final Check B

Listening

A. Listen to the recording, then fill in the gaps with one word.

Meg tried to 1) .... Belle's offer, but Belle insisted that she would make Meg into a true 2) .... So, on Thursday evening, Belle and her maid 3) .... Meg's hair, fastened her dress very tightly and put silver 4) .... on her. When Meg was finally ready, the Moffat sisters were all 5) .... at how beautiful she looked, and they led her into the 6) .... room. Everyone turned as Meg walked into the room. They all wanted to know who the beautiful young lady was. Meg felt very 7) .... by all the attention. She played with her 8) .... and chatted and laughed with a young 9) .... who tried to amuse her. Suddenly, she saw Laurie on the other side of the room and went to 10) .... him.

10x2=20

20

Story

B. Put the following events in the correct chronological order.

1 ... a Meg receives a love letter.
2 ... b Beth gets scarlet fever.
3 ... c Jo goes to a newspaper to try and publish two stories.
4 ... d Mrs March goes to Washington
5 ... e Meg goes to stay with the Moffats for a week.

5x3=15

15

C. **Explain what you think was meant by the following.**

1 Chapter 9, p. 57: *"Don't be silly, Laurie. If I talk to your grandfather and ask him to apologize for getting so angry with you, will you forget about running away?"*
   ....

2 Chapter 10, p. 58: *"Here's another present for the March family."*
   ....

3 Chapter 10, p. 63: *"I will marry whoever I like."*
   ....

3x10=30

30

New Words

D. **Fill in the gaps with a word from the box.**

| respected nervous defended symptoms rules |

1 When Amy brought limes to school, she broke the ....
2 Meg felt very .... when she was alone with Mr Brooke.
3 Mrs March wanted her daughters to be ....
4 Meg .... John against Aunt March.
5 Beth had the .... of scarlet fever.

5x3=15

15

E. *Fill in the gaps with the correct form of the words in capitals.*

1 Amy didn't hear Laurie's .... and skated where the ice was smooth.   WARN
2 Mr Davis hit Amy with his ruler as a ....   PUNISH
3 Jo was not happy about Meg's .... to John.   MARRY
4 Aunt March talked to Meg in a .... tone of voice.   THREATEN
5 Amy was .... punished by her teacher.   SEVERE

5x4=20

20

✓ Key to Final Check A

NB: *The listening section is taken from Chapter 5.*

A 1 insisted   4 ready   7 attention   10 side
   2 maid   5 led   8 chatted
   3 fastened   6 turned   9 amuse

B 1 c   2 a   3 b   4 e   5 d

C (Suggested answers)
   1 Chapter 1, p. 13:
      Beth finds it hard to believe when she sees their table covered with all sorts of delicacies and decorated with colourful flowers. In the last few days, the atmosphere in the March house has been rather gloomy, as the girls have had nothing to look forward to. The surprise they get from Mr Laurence keeps the Christmas spirit alive and brings the children joy personified as Father Christmas.
   2 Chapter 6, p. 41:
      Jo proves to be very generous. Not only does she not regret what she has done but she is willing to do it again to help anyone in the family. However, now that she is alone with Meg, she can't hide her sadness about her hair, and her eyes fill with tears.
   3 Chapter 9, p. 53:
      Meg is obviously embarrassed to have received a love letter. She is too young and inexperienced to be familiar with this sort of situation. Her first reaction is to get upset and think Jo and Laurie are playing a joke on her.

D 1 confirmed   3 ashamed   5 elegant
   2 library   4 hospitable

E 1 generosity   3 apology   5 childish
   2 occasionally 4 envious

Key to Final Check B

NB: *The listening section is taken from Chapter 5.*

A 1 refuse   4 jewelry   7 flattered   10 greet
   2 beauty   5 delighted 8 fan
   3 curled   6 drawing   9 gentleman

B 1 e   2 c   3 d   4 b   5 a

C (**Suggested answers**)
   1 Chapter 9, p. 57:
     Jo is trying to make Laurie act sensibly and not run away. She offers to help clear the misunderstanding between him and his grandfather, proving to be more mature and determined than Laurie.
   2 Chapter 10, p. 58:
     Laurie is enjoying the festive atmosphere at the March house, participating in the family's joy. Like a little boy, he can't wait to see their reaction when Mr March walks into the room after a whole year. He doesn't reveal the good news, though, but he is secretly preparing the family for a big surprise.
   3 Chapter 10, p. 63:
     Only a few moments earlier, Meg felt so nervous and embarrassed that she could hardly say a word to John. Now, her aunt's threats, showing complete disregard for Meg's feelings, make Meg so angry that she finds the courage to stand up to her and confront her, appearing to be quite bold.

D 1 rules   3 respected   5 symptoms
   2 nervous   4 defended

E 1 warning   3 marriage   5 severely
   2 punishment   4 threatening

THINK! Activities

Chapter 3

Write down three advantages and three disadvantages, both for having brothers and sisters and for being an only child. Compare your ideas with the rest of the class. Then say which situation you would prefer to be in, giving reasons.

'Jo felt lucky to have three sisters to talk to, and she felt sorry for Laurie, who had no brothers or sisters at all.'

Chapter 5

Complete the sentences so that they are true for you.

1 It is important for a family to ....
   ....
2 Snobbish people ....
   ....
3 If someone is poor, ...
   ....
4 It is very rude to ....
   ....
5 The best way to earn someone's respect is ....
   ....
6 A good friend is someone who ....
   ....

Chapter 6

What evidence can you find in Chapter 6 of *Little Women* that it is a 19th century novel? Make a list. Then suggest how a modern writer might convey the same things, e.g. travelling on an omnibus >travelling on the Underground.

Chapter 8

Complete the sentences so that they are true for you.

1 Women should ....
....
2 Falling in love ....
....
3 Marriage is ....
....
4 Money can be ....
....
5 Happiness is something ....
....
6 Working hard means that ....
....

Suggested Answers for the THINK! Activities

Chapter 3
(Any three from each of the following categories)

	Brothers & sisters	Only child
ADVANTAGES	• sb to share your problems with • get help with homework, etc • do things together • share clothes, toys, etc	• no siblings to fight with • don't have to compete for attention • more choices/opportunities • better start in life
DISADVANTAGES	• less attention from parents • fewer material possessions • lack of privacy • reduced schooling opportunities	• under more pressure from parents • get lonely/bored • might become bossy/spoiled • lack of family support at an older age

Chapter 5

1 ... support each other at all times.
2 ... think that they are better than others.
3 ... that doesn't mean they don't have dignity.
4 ... not say thank you when someone does you a favour.
5 ... to be honest and kind.
6 ... never lets you down.

Chapter 6

- Jo hopes no one will see her taking her stories to the newspaper office.
- Mr Brooke keeps Meg's glove in his pocket.
- The March family receive a telegram.
- Laurie fetches his carriage and horses to go and leave a note at Aunt March's.
- Jo sells her hair to a wigmaker.

In a modern novel, a woman writer would not need to keep her work secret, as writing today is considered a perfectly respectable occupation for a woman, in contrast with 19th century views. A modern Mr Brooke would probably have Meg's mobile phone number in his phone as proof of romantic attachment. People today no longer receive urgent news via a telegram; they receive a phone call or an SMS. Also, if someone needed to go somewhere today they wouldn't ride a carriage. Lastly, if someone wanted to raise money, they would not sell their hair, as wigs have gone out of fashion. They would be more likely to sell a luxury item, e.g. jewellery or electronic equipment.

Chapter 8

1 ... always try to develop their personal talents.
2 ... is a wonderful experience.
3 ... not what you always expect.
4 ... very useful at times.
5 ... you don't always recognise even when you have it.
6 ... you become more independent and self-reliant.

Board Game Questions and Suggested Answers

1 When does the story take place?
 The story takes place in the 1860s, during the American Civil War.
2 Where is Mr March during most of the story?
 Mr March is away fighting in the American Civil War.
3 Why aren't the Marches going to have presents for Christmas this year?
 They are too poor, and their mother says they shouldn't spend money on pleasurable things while the men are suffering in the war.
4 Who is the oldest sister?
 Meg is the oldest.
5 Who is the youngest sister?
 Amy is the youngest.
6 What do the girls want to buy their mother?
 They want to buy her a pair of slippers.
7 What do the four sisters promise after they read their father's letter?
 They promise to become better.
8 What does Father talk about in his first letter home to the family?
 He talks about his love for his wife and daughters.
9 What do the sisters find under their pillows on Christmas morning?
 Each one finds a different coloured book from Mother.
10 Where does the March family go on Christmas morning?
 They go to the Hummels' house.
11 How do the March girls spend Christmas night?
 They perform a play.
12 Who do the March sisters receive a gift from on Christmas night?
 They receive a gift from Mr Laurence.

13 What surprise do the girls get after performing the play?
   They find the table covered with ice cream, cake, fruit and sweets.
14 Who does Beth think about when she looks at the flowers Mr Laurence sent the girls?
   She thinks about her father.
15 Where are Jo and Meg invited to?
   They are invited to a New Year's Eve party.
16 Why is Jo supposed to keep her back out of sight at the New Year's Eve party?
   Because her only nice dress has a burn and a tear in the back.
17 What is wrong with Jo's gloves?
   She spilled lemonade on them and now they are ruined.
18 What happens to Meg's hair while she is getting ready for the party?
   It gets burned while Jo is trying to curl it.
19 Why does Meg feel uncomfortable before she leaves for the New Year's Eve party?
   Because her shoes are too tight.
20 Why does Jo feel uncomfortable before she leaves for the New Year's Eve party?
   Because her hair pins are sticking into her head.
21 Why does Jo want to hide at the New Year's Eve party?
   She feels shy when she sees a boy coming to ask her to dance.
22 Who is Theodore Laurence?
   He is the Marches' next door neighbour, Mr Laurence's grandson.
23 How do the girls solve Meg's hair problem for the New Year's Eve party?
   They tie her hair in a ribbon so that the damage doesn't show too much.
24 Who gives Meg and Jo a ride home after the New Year's Eve party?
   Laurie gives them a ride home in his grandfather's carriage.
25 What happens to Meg at the New Year's Eve party?
   Her shoe turns and she twists her ankle.

26 How does Mr March lose all of his property?
He tries to help an unfortunate friend.
27 What do Meg and Jo ask their parents when their father loses his property?
They beg their parents to let them work so that they can help the family.
28 What job does Jo have?
Jo looks after old Aunt March.
29 What job does Meg have?
She works as a nursery governess.
30 How does Jo get along with Aunt March?
She gets along quite well with Aunt March, although they occasionally argue.
31 How does Jo pass her time at Aunt March's?
She reads books in Aunt March's library.
32 Who does Mr March give lessons to before leaving home?
He gives lessons to Beth.
33 Why does Beth study at home?
Because she is too shy to go to school.
34 Who does Beth help while at home?
She helps Hannah take care of the house.
35 What does Beth long for at home?
She longs for a good piano because the one they have is old and tuneless.
36 Why can't Beth have a new piano at home?
Because there's no money for such luxuries in the March house.
37 Where does Beth often go to play the piano?
She goes to the Laurence house next door.
38 Why does Amy's teacher complain?
Because Amy draws animals in her school books, instead of doing her sums.
39 Who has to wear their cousin's old clothes?
Amy.
40 What is Amy admired for at school?
She is admired for her grace and talent.

41 Who is Jo closest to of all her sisters?
Jo is closest to Beth.
42 When does Jo start visiting Laurie?
After New Year, when Laurie has a bad cold and can't go out.
43 How does Mr Laurence know the March family?
Mr Laurence knew Mrs March's father many years ago.
44 Why does Meg want to visit the Laurence house?
Because she wants to walk in the conservatory.
45 What is Beth's gift to Mr Laurence?
A pair of slippers.
46 What does Mr Laurence send Beth in return for her gift?
He sends her a piano.
47 Why does Meg give money to Amy?
Amy needs to buy pickled limes to pay back the other girls at school.
48 How much money does Meg give to Amy to buy the limes?
Meg gives Amy about twenty-five cents.
49 Where does Amy keep her limes at school?
She keeps them in her desk.
50 How does the teacher find out that Amy has pickled limes?
Jenny Snow, one of Amy's classmates, tells the teacher.
51 What does Amy do after she gets into trouble at school?
She runs home and tells her mother and sisters.
52 Why doesn't Amy go to the theatre with Meg, Jo and Laurie?
Only Meg and Jo are invited, and Jo says that it would be rude to bring Amy along too.
53 How does Jo react when she finds out that Amy threw her book into the fire?
She becomes very upset and tells Amy she'll never forgive her.
54 What was Jo's book about?
It was a book of fairy tales.
55 Where does Jo go the day after her argument with Amy?
She goes ice skating on the river with Laurie.
56 What does Amy do when Jo and Laurie go ice skating?
She follows Jo and Laurie to the river.

57 How does Jo feel after Amy falls into the river?
She feels guilty and blames her bad temper for Amy's accident.
58 What does Mrs March tell Jo regarding her own temper?
Mrs March says that her own temper used to be as bad as Jo's.
59 How does Jo react to her mother revealing that she used to get angry?
She is surprised because Mrs March never looks angry.
60 What happens when Amy opens her eyes after the ice skating accident?
Jo and she hug each other and make up.
61 Where does Meg stay for a fortnight?
She stays with Annie Moffat and her family.
62 What is Mrs March afraid of when Meg is about to leave?
She is afraid that Meg will enjoy fashionable life and not want to return to her simple life.
63 How does Meg realise that the Moffat sisters pity her?
As they are getting ready for a party, Meg notices the way they are looking at her shabby old dress.
64 How does Meg feel when she stays with the Moffats?
At first Meg is happy to act like a rich, sophisticated person but slowly she feels out of place.
65 What does Laurie send Meg while she is at the Moffat house?
He sends her a bouquet of roses.
66 What does Laurie think of Meg when he sees her at the Moffat house?
He thinks she doesn't look like herself because of the way she is dressed.
67 How does Meg find out what the Moffats really think of her?
She overhears the Moffat sisters chatting with their mother.
68 What does Belle Moffat do to make Meg beautiful for a ball?
She gives Meg her blue silk dress and jewellery to wear and, with her maid, they curl Meg's hair.
69 What makes Meg wish she had worn her own clothes?
She hears two of the guests saying she looks like a doll to dress up and play with.

70 Why does Meg say that she behaved like a fool too?
She says this because she enjoyed being admired by everyone at the party.
71 What does Meg do while the other sisters play with Laurie?
She chats with Mr Brooke, Laurie's teacher.
72 Where does Jo go after putting two sets of papers in her pocket?
She goes to a newspaper editor's office.
73 Where does Laurie think Jo is going when he sees her going up and down the stairs of a building?
Laurie thinks that Jo is going to a dentist's surgery.
74 Who is Laurie's secret about?
Laurie's secret is about Meg and Mr Brooke.
75 Apart from having her stories published, what other good news does Jo receive from the newspaper?
They will pay her to write more stories for them.
76 What bad news arrives shortly after Jo's stories are printed?
A telegram comes that says Mr March is very ill and that Mrs March should go to Washington immediately.
77 How does Mr Brooke help Mrs March after she receives the telegram?
He escorts her to Washington and stays there until Mr March recovers.
78 How does Laurie help when the Marches receive the bad news about Mr March?
He goes and informs Aunt March.
79 What does Jo do to help her father when he becomes ill?
She sells her hair to a man who makes wigs.
80 How do Beth and Amy pass their time when their mother is away in Washington?
Beth and Amy help Hannah around the house.
81 What does Meg do every day while her mother is away?
Meg goes and teaches the King children.
82 Why can't Jo work when her mother is away?
Because she catches a cold.
83 Who does Beth visit regularly while her mother is gone?
Beth visits the Hummel family.

84 What is wrong with Beth after she comes back from the Hummel house one evening?
Beth comes home sick with scarlet fever.
85 What are Beth's symptoms?
She's got a headache and a sore throat.
86 Why don't the girls tell Mrs March about Beth's illness?
Hannah doesn't want to overburden their mother with worry.
87 Where does Amy go while Beth is ill?
Amy goes to stay with Aunt March.
88 How does Mrs March find out about Beth's illness?
Laurie sends her a message.
89 What do Meg and Jo realise while Beth is ill?
They realise that love and health are much more important than money or beauty.
90 How does Jo feel when Laurie sends for her mother in Washington?
She is glad and relieved.
91 Why are the girls worried by their mother's delay?
They are worried that their mother won't reach them before Beth dies.
92 How does Beth's face look different the night she starts recovering from her illness?
It looks pale and peaceful, not flushed with fever anymore.
93 Why is Hannah laughing and crying at the same time after Jo kisses Beth, who is ill in bed?
Hannah realises that Beth is going to live.
94 What does the doctor say after he examines Beth for the very last time?
He agrees with Hannah that Beth is going to be fine.
95 Where is Amy when Beth first wakes up from the fever?
Amy is still staying with Aunt March.
96 Why does Mr Brooke stay in Washington when Mrs March comes home?
He stays in Washington to take care of Mr March.
97 What delays Mrs March getting back home to see Beth?
A storm delays her journey home.

98 What does Amy tell Mrs March when the latter visits her daughter at Aunt March's?
Amy tells her mother lots of stories about her time with her aunt.
99 What realisation does Amy come to when her mother returns from Washington?
She realises that she has been a selfish girl.
100 Why is Jo worried about Meg falling in love with Mr Brooke?
Jo is worried that Mr Brooke will take Meg away from them.
101 Why doesn't Mrs March want Meg to get engaged yet?
She feels that Meg is still too young to get married.
102 When does Mrs March want Meg to get married?
She wants her to wait until she is at least 20 years old.
103 What does Mrs March suggest they do when Jo tells her about Meg and Mr Brooke?
She suggests they wait until Mr March comes back.
104 How does Laurie feel when they find out about his joke?
He feels ashamed and regretful.
105 How does Laurie feel when Jo refuses to forgive him?
He is very hurt.
106 Who does Laurie want to take with him when he decides to run away from home?
He wants to take Jo with him.
107 When does Laurie stop thinking about running away to Washington?
When Jo talks to his grandfather and gets him to apologise to Laurie.
108 What surprise do Jo and Laurie have for Beth on Christmas day?
They have made a snow woman in the garden.
109 How does everyone greet Mr March when he arrives home?
They run and hug him.
110 What does Beth do when she hears everyone's cries of excitement the day Mr March returns?
She jumps out of bed and rushes into her father's arms.
111 Who joins the March family for Christmas dinner?
The Laurences and Mr Brooke.

112 What does Mr March say to his daughters after Christmas dinner when the guests have left?
He praises them for their bravery and their achievements while he was away.

113 What can Mr March tell looking at Meg's hands?
They are not as smooth as they were, which means she's been working hard.

114 How is Jo different when her father sees her again after a year?
She is not boyish and wild but has become a young lady.

115 When does Mr Brooke come to visit the March house alone?
The day after Mr March's return.

116 How does Meg feel when she is alone with Mr Brooke?
At first she is nervous and just mumbles but then she gets very excited and tells him to leave.

115 Who interrupts Meg and Mr Brooke's private conversation?
Aunt March, who has come to welcome back Mr March.

118 What does Aunt March say to Meg regarding Mr Brooke?
She tells her to marry a rich man instead of Mr Brooke, and even threatens that she won't leave her any money if she doesn't listen to her.

119 How does Meg react to Aunt March's advice regarding Mr Brooke?
Meg gets angry and stands up to her aunt, defending Mr Brooke.

120 Why does Jo eventually sound pleased?
Because she sees everyone in the family so happy.

Suggested Explanations for the Picture Cards

There are several ways the picture cards for the *Little Women* Board Game may be related to the story. Here are the most obvious ones:

1. The **fireplace** = The place where the Marches gather and spend time together. / The place where Amy throws and burns Jo's book of stories.
2. The **ruler** = The ruler that Amy's teacher hits her palm with to punish her for bringing pickled limes to school.
3. The **wig** = Jo's hair that she sells to a man who makes wigs to get money for her father.
4. The **icy river** = The river where Jo and Laurie go skating followed by Amy, who almost drowns.
5. The **box of roses and the note** = The ones Mrs March and Laurie send to Meg while she stays at the Moffats.
6. The **books of music** = The ones Mr Laurence leaves on his piano for Meg to find.
7. The **bottle of medicine** = The one Beth is holding when Jo finds her sitting on the medicine chest.
8. The **writing book and pen** = What Jo uses to write her stories.
9. The **love letter** = The one sent to Meg by Laurie, who signs as Mr Brooke.
10. The **limes** = The ones Amy secretly takes to school and gets punished for.
11. The **turquoise ring** = The one Aunt March gives Amy as a gift while Amy is staying at her house.
12. The **stained gloves** = Jo's gloves that she can't wear to the New Year's Eve party because they are stained with lemonade.
13. The **medical book** = Mrs March's medical book that Beth looks at to find she has the symptoms of scarlet fever.
14. The **Daily News sign** = The newspaper office Jo visits to drop in her stories.
15. The **evening gown** = The one Belle Moffat lends Meg to wear to a party.

16 The **library** = The room Jo is especially fond of at Aunt March's house.
17 The **bundle of banknotes** = The money Jo earns when she sells her hair to a wigmaker.
18 The **slippers** = The ones Beth makes for Mr Laurence to thank him for letting her play on his piano.

QUESTION CARDS

1. Who are the March sisters?
   They are Meg, Jo, Beth and Amy.
2. Who comforts Jo when she cries about her hair?
   Meg comforts her.
3. What does Beth like doing in her spare time?
   She likes playing the piano.
4. What does Mr Brooke want by the end of the story?
   He wants to marry Meg.
5. Where do Meg and Jo go on New Year's Eve?
   They go to a party at Mrs Gardiner's house.

---

1. What solution does Jo find to the "gloves problem"?
   Jo says Meg and she can each wear one of Meg's gloves and carry one of Jo's stained gloves in their other hand.
2. What is Laurie's real name?
   Theodore.
3. Why does the Laurence boy want to be called Laurie?
   He doesn't like his real name.
4. What family does Meg work for?
   Meg works for the King family.
5. What does Aunt March give Amy as a gift?
   A turquoise ring.

---

1. Why does Amy refuse to give Jenny Snow a lime?
   Because Jenny has been very unfriendly to Amy before.
2. Who is Meg closest to of all her sisters?
   Meg is closest to Amy.
3. Why does Jo feel sorry for Laurie?
   Because he has no brothers or sisters to talk to.
4. Who used to play on the Laurence piano before Beth?
   Mr Laurence's granddaughter.
5. How does Jo spend her free time?
   Reading and writing.

---

1. What is Amy's talent?
   She is talented at drawing.
2. How is Amy's life in danger at some point in the story?
   Amy falls into the river while ice skating and almost drowns.
3. Who gives Jo advice regarding her temper?
   Her mother.
4. Who is the love letter addressed to?
   It is addressed to Meg.
5. Why is Amy punished at school?
   Because she brings pickled limes, which is against the rules.

QUESTION CARDS

QUESTION CARDS

QUESTION CARDS

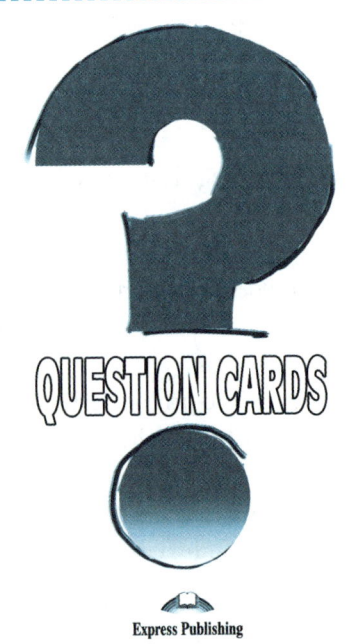

QUESTION CARDS

1. Where are Jo and Laurie when he tells her about his secret?
   They are outside the newspaper office.
2. Who is Hannah?
   She is the Marches' servant.
3. Who thinks that poor girls don't stand a chance?
   Belle Moffat thinks so.
4. What are Meg's symptoms of being in love?
   She doesn't sleep, doesn't eat and sits in corners, day-dreaming.
5. Why does Laurie hide at the New Year's Eve party?
   Because he doesn't know many people around and feels strange.

1. Who does Meg think the love letter she receives is from?
   She thinks it's from Mr Brooke.
2. When does Jo first meet Laurie?
   When the Marches' cat runs away and Laurie brings it back, she chats with him over the fence.
3. Who does Jo want Meg to marry?
   She wants Meg to marry Laurie.
4. Who does Meg chat with at the New Year's Eve party?
   Meg chats with a group of girls.
5. Who writes a fake love letter to Meg?
   Laurie writes a letter to Meg, signing it as Mr Brooke.

1. What makes Laurie want to run away from home?
   An argument he has with his grandfather.
2. Who escorts Mrs March to Washington?
   Mr Brooke.
3. When does Mr Brooke realise that Meg really loves him?
   When she defends him against Aunt March.
4. How do Meg and Jo come back home from Mrs Gardiner's party?
   In Mr Laurence's carriage.
5. Who does Beth see first when she wakes from the fever?
   She sees her mother.

1. Why does Laurie say his grandfather won't apologise to him after they argue?
   Because he is too stubborn.
2. What does Mr Brooke plan to do before asking Meg to marry him?
   He plans to earn enough money to buy a nice house.
3. What are the sisters doing by the fire at the beginning of the story?
   They are knitting and talking about Christmas.
4. How long does Meg stay with the Moffats?
   For a fortnight.
5. Who is Mr Brooke?
   He is Laurie's tutor.

QUESTION CARDS

Express Publishing

QUESTION CARDS

Express Publishing

QUESTION CARDS

Express Publishing

QUESTION CARDS

Express Publishing

1. What does Laurie call Jo when he sees her at Mrs Gardiner's party?
He calls her Miss March.
2. Who do the sisters give their breakfast to on Christmas day?
They give their breakfast to the Hummel family.
3. What is Aunt March like?
Aunt March is a grumpy old lady.
4. How does Meg spend her time with the Moffats?
She attends dinners, goes to the theatre and goes shopping.
5. Where does Laurie want to run away to?
He wants to go to Washington.

1. Why does Jo leave the house in secrecy one day?
She goes to see a newspaper editor about her stories.
2. Why is Jo not pleased to hear Laurie's secret?
She doesn't want Mr Brooke to take Meg away.
3. Why can't Mr Laurence escort Mrs March to Washington?
Because he is too old for such a long journey.
4. Why does Jo cry the night before Mrs March leaves for Washington?
She is sad that she cut her hair.
5. What does Beth become ill with?
She becomes ill with scarlet fever.

1. How does Amy's teacher punish her?
He hits her hand with a ruler and makes her stand at the front of the class.
2. What does Amy do when Jo refuses to take her to the theatre?
She throws Jo's book of fairy tales into the fire.
3. How does Amy fall into the river?
She skates on smooth ice.
4. Who are the Moffat sisters?
They are Sallie, Belle and Clara.
5. Why does Amy go to stay at Aunt March's?
So that she doesn't get scarlet fever from Beth.

1. Who takes care of Beth while she is ill?
Hannah, Jo and Meg.
2. How does Laurie know Meg and Mr Brooke are in love?
He sees Meg's glove in Mr Brooke's pocket.
3. Who brings Mrs March home when she returns from Washington?
Laurie.
4. Where was Louisa May Alcott born?
She was born in Pennsylvania, USA.
5. How does Beth thank Mr Laurence for letting her play on his piano?
She makes him a pair of slippers.

QUESTION CARDS

Express Publishing

QUESTION CARDS

Express Publishing

QUESTION CARDS

Express Publishing

QUESTION CARDS

Express Publishing

PICTURE CARDS

1
2
3
4
5
6

99

PICTURE CARDS

Express Publishing

PICTURE CARDS

Express Publishing

PICTURE CARDS

Express Publishing

PICTURE CARDS

Express Publishing

PICTURE CARDS

Express Publishing

PICTURE CARDS

Express Publishing

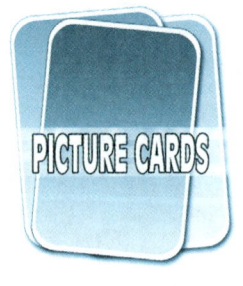

101

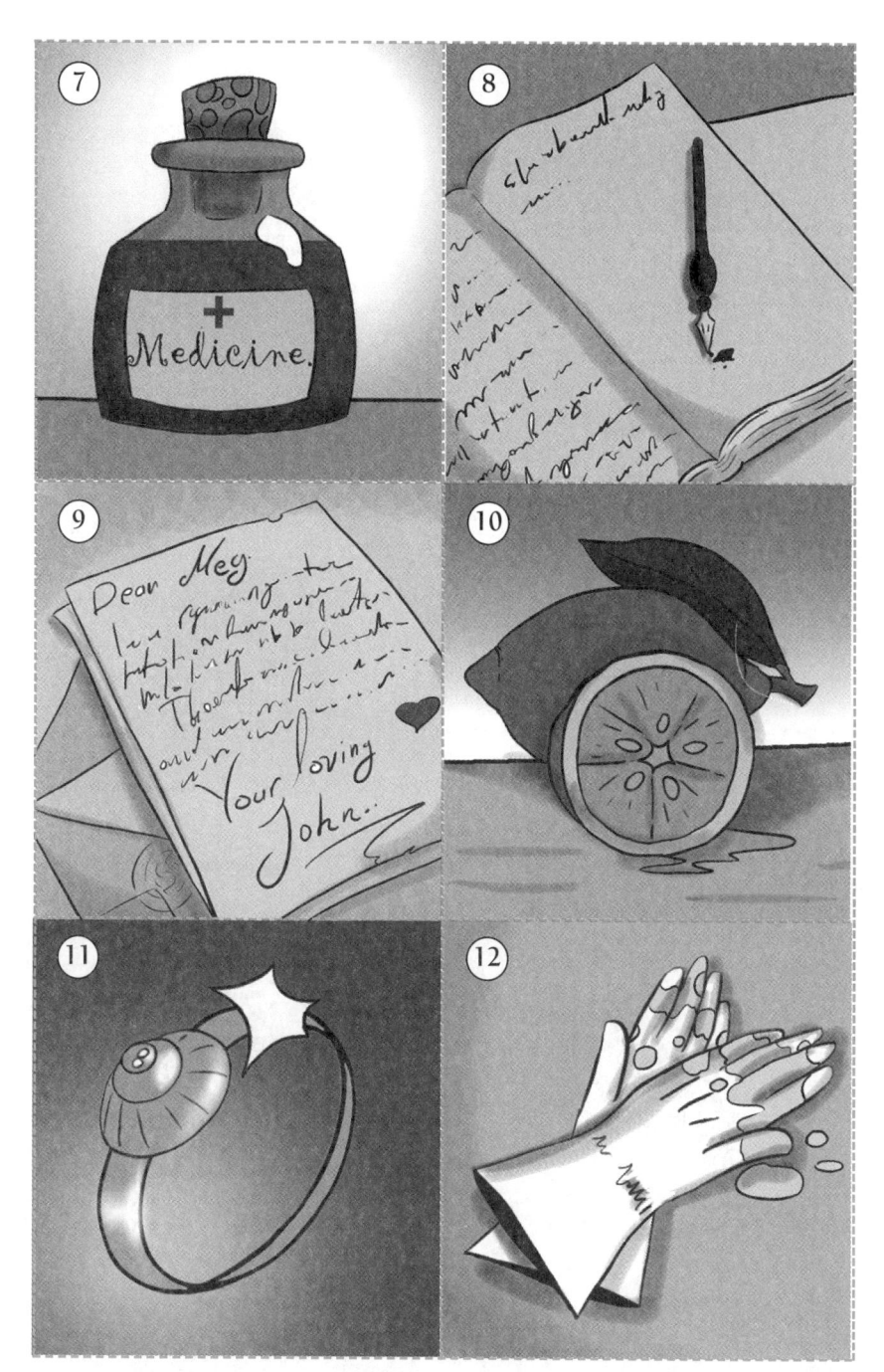

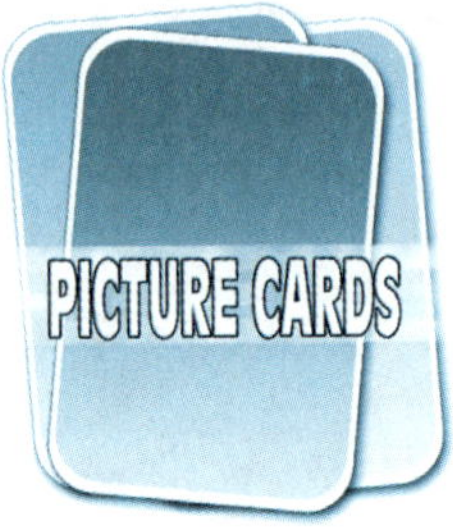

Express Publishing

Express Publishing

Express Publishing

Express Publishing

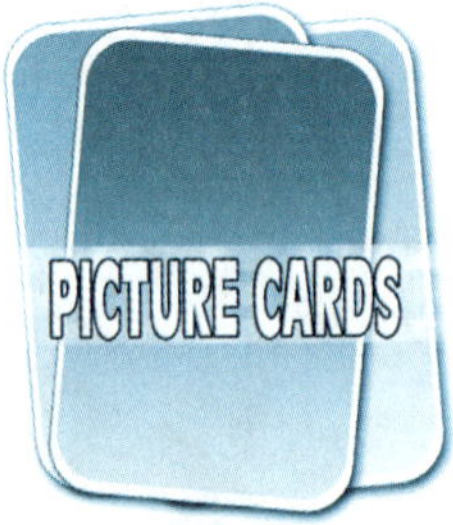

Express Publishing

Express Publishing

13. Medical Science

14. Daily News

15.

16.

17.

18.

PICTURE CARDS

Express Publishing

PICTURE CARDS

Express Publishing

PICTURE CARDS

Express Publishing

PICTURE CARDS

Express Publishing

PICTURE CARDS

Express Publishing

PICTURE CARDS

Express Publishing

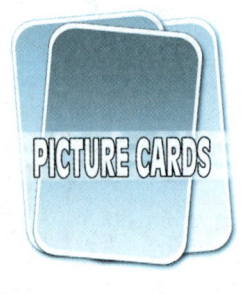

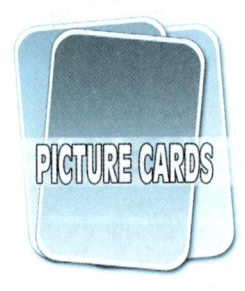

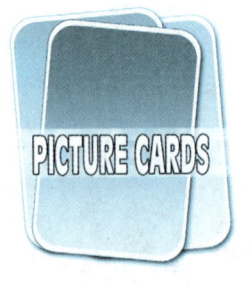

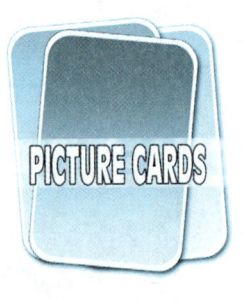